A Higher

Ransom

A Higher Ransom

ALEIGHA C. ISRAEL

A LIGHT FOR CHRIST TRILOGY

In Loving Memory of
Mr. Faske,
a true soldier and light for Christ.
Your testimony and love for others has
touched the lives of many.
You will never be forgotten...

...and Dedicated to

my Heavenly Savior, whose life inspired me
to write this story. His life of perfect love and
unconditional sacrifice brings me
encouragement every day. Thank You, Lord,
for never tiring of hearing my prayers, for
never leaving or forsaking me.

Thank You for being my perfect ransom—
a much higher ransom than I will ever
deserve.

"For even the Son of Man did not come to be served, but to serve, and to give His life a ransom for many."

Mark 10:45

Acknowledgments

I must say this book would be nothing without the help, direction and guidance of my Heavenly Father. It would have been a book not worth reading, a book that lacked so much. But because of Him, an idea and story plot have been turned into a reality.

I want to thank my parents. Without their help and encouragement this book would have probably not been finished. Thank you both for taking the time to read and edit my book. Thank you, Mama and Daddy!

My dear siblings, thank you for your enraptured interest and kind advice. Thank you for celebrating with me and sharing in my enjoyment when this book was finally finished!

Nana and Papa, thank you so much for your loving encouragement while I was writing this book. Your interest and excitement helped me to press forward when I hit a bump in the road. Thank you so much!

Omie and Grandpa, thank you for the ideas you gave while I was looking for pictures for my cover. And thank you for referring me to Lindsay McDonald. That was by far the best reference I have ever been given!

Aunt Leisha, I can't thank you enough for my fabulous covers. You went over and beyond my expectations. Thank you so much!

My beta readers and YWW family,
I don't know what I did before I joined the Young Writer's Workshop community. More accurately, I don't know what I'd do *without* you! Each one of you has a special place in my heart!

Lindsay McDonald, words can never express my thanks to you for editing this book and the amazing interior design you did as well. You were an answer to my prayers and so much more! You will never know how thankful I am to have met you.

Dear reader, may you be blessed and encouraged by the story within these pages.

Laus Deo!

Aleigha C. Israel

Prologue

Eighteen-year-old Anna Haddington pressed a hand to her stiff back as she rose from her crouched position on the damp, stone floor.

The unmistakable *click-click* of the King's ornate shoes grew louder as he approached.

What was that scuffling sound? He rounded the corner, his hands clasping Lilly's behind her back.

Lilly's young dark-skinned face was etched with fear and her eyes were large, seeming to echo the feeling that washed over Anna's soul.

"Yes, aren't I nice?" King Raymond laughed, the sound sending chills up Anna's spine. "I brought your little friend to visit you!"

Anna's stomach churned and her hands trembled, palms growing sweaty. "What do you want with her?"

"It is not her I want, it's *you*."

Anna's brow crinkled in confusion. "But what does she have to do with—" she stopped suddenly as she began to understand.

"Yes, I think you understand now," the king's sly tone was edged with something Anna couldn't quite place.

But dangerous. Very, very dangerous.

Anna prayed her intuition was wrong, but where the King was concerned, one could never be too careful.

He stepped up to the edge of her cell and wrapped his fingers around the black lock, keeping hold of Lilly with his free hand.

The soft *click* of the key settling into the lock echoed through the cold, dark prison, seeming to seal Anna's fate.

"You have three days to recant, or she dies!"

Raymond gave Lilly a slight shake and her eyes filled with intense fright.

This is too much! Anna thought as King Raymond opened the door of her cell and roughly shoved Lilly inside.

Anna caught Lilly before she landed on the hard, stone floor.

This is all my fault, Anna thought, the young woman limp in her arms. She had prepared herself for the death she knew was to come to her, but now Lilly's life was being threatened.

I don't know what to do, Lord! Anna begged silently, tears streaming down her face. *Please show me the way!*

One

Three months earlier
Carpathia, *1849*

Anna Haddington took a deep breath of salty air. Carpathia was her stop—her last stop to her new destination, the place that would soon be her home.

Anna brushed aside her dark brown tresses as the wind whipped them about her face.

Children ran around the ship's deck in a lively game of tag and everyone felt the relief and joy of finally reaching land.

They had arrived and docked safely at the coast of Carpathia.

Anna picked up her satchel and walked to the stern of the ship. Her gaze drifted absently out over the sea, not focusing on the rolling hills and snow-capped mountains, but trying to sort through all the events of the past few months.

It was startling how much could happen in such a short time.

Almost a year ago, she had lived in a small cottage in France with her dear parents and three precious siblings. But shortly after Isaiah was born, her mother died, causing much grief to them all. They had somehow managed to flow gently back into their daily routine of life and had even found things to laugh about again.

So much had happened since even then. The past three weeks alone had gone by so rapidly, she hadn't even had time to think through all of it properly until now.

Her father had been weak and ill for many months. She should have suspected that he was sick, but maybe she was too naïve to understand. Or perhaps she just didn't allow herself.

Anna's chin trembled as she thought of her father. He was so loving and gentle and always smiling. Up until the days his sickness overtook him, he had been a very hard worker. As a farmer, there were many chores that needed his attention; milking the cows, tending to the hen house, butchering the poultry. It seemed that every season brought in a new addition to the farm, and with that, more responsibilities.

Her father loved the Lord with all his heart. She knew without a doubt that he was in heaven right now, with her mother, rejoicing before the feet of their Savior.

They had never been poor, though they had lived a very humble life, not wasting money on frivolous things. Because their father was unable to work those last few months, their supply of money had slowly run out. She had offered to take a job in town, but he wouldn't allow it.

"The Lord shall provide, Anna dear. He always has and He always will."

She wished she had his faith.

Tears fell as she thought of the brothers and sisters she had left behind. Her brother Caleb had just turned ten. She remembered how even at a young age, he had such a fire for Christ. He would share God's love with everyone he met. Most notably, he had been trying to witness to a young Muslim girl named Amira Anna knew that Caleb would never stop witnessing to Amira and sharing God's love.

She thought of her sisters, Margret and Julianna. They had made her parting much harder than she would have chosen. Their sweet personalities and the fun times they had shared would never be forgotten. And then there was the baby of the family, Isaiah. His smile and bubbly personality had been a joy to them all.

After both of their parents' deaths, the children had been separated and split between two families within the church.

At eighteen years of age, Anna could have been a lot of help to many families, but the Lord seemed to have had other plans. Soon after her father's death, she received a letter from her aunt in Carpathia. After hearing of his death, Aunt Jane wanted to help in any way that she possibly could. She offered Anna a place to stay within her home and sent money for passage to come and live with her, along with a few coins for extra expenses. At any other time and place, Anna would have said no at once, but now, after everything that had happened, she was inclined to say yes, though she knew she could not answer such an important letter without consulting her Heavenly Father. After much prayer and consideration, she replied, letting her aunt know when to expect her. She had never been on a ship before, and the preparations took her a few days. She almost changed her mind just before leaving, but something deep within her told her that this was the right decision.

Now, she was gone, and there was no turning back. She would live with her aunt and try to start a new life—a life, she hoped, that would make her parents proud.

Everything would turn out better from here, right? She'd felt peace about her decision, and God knew best, didn't He?

Anna chided herself for even thinking of doubting God's guidance and direction. She decided from now on that she would try her best not to doubt God and His plans. He knew what was best for her life and she would fully trust Him. Whatever happened, she knew she was under His sovereign care and mercy.

As she made her way towards the front of the ship, she walked with a new reassurance, a reassurance that everything was going to be fine. A quiet peace settled over Anna as she remembered a verse in Romans:

> *"And we know that all things work together for good to them that love God, to them who are the called according to His purpose."*

Anna walked down the ship's ramp, scanning the crowd of people for her aunt.

"Watch your step!" warned a pleasant-faced man, nodding to the slight drop-off at the foot of the ramp.

"*Merci*, sir." Anna gave him a quiet smile.

"My pleasure, Miss," he replied, with a touch of his hat.

Anna set her luggage down and looked around the dock, not exactly sure as to what or whom she was looking for. Did Aunt Jane say she would meet Anna here? Maybe she was going to send someone.

The sun had started its daily descent down the mountain and a slight chill was coming with it. She picked up her bag and decided to step into the small building that served as both a waiting room and a ticket office. Once inside, she felt a drastic change. It was quiet indoors, and only then did she realize how loud it had been outside.

The room was toasty warm and it smelled slightly of coffee.

The only other occupants in the room were two ladies, one of whom sat in the corner and the other a few feet away from Anna. A rather grumpy looking man stood behind the ticket counter.

She sat down in a chair close to the window and told herself not to worry. *Auntie will be here soon.*

However, deep down, she felt a twinge of anxiety. *I must trust!*

But it was so hard. Her thoughts flew quickly to a verse in John.

"Peace I leave with you: My peace I give unto you: not as the world giveth, give I unto you. Let not your heart be troubled, neither let it be afraid."

She glanced out the window. People were coming and going, picking up and dropping off their loved ones. Everywhere she looked there were horses, wagons and buggies. A family stood off to the side, offering tearful goodbyes to a young lady whom Anna assumed was their daughter. The young lady hugged a small child who had flung his arms around her neck. Anna watched as the father and mother embraced the woman, and it was then she realized how much she missed the embrace of her own dear parents. She also knew how hard it was to leave a loved one behind, not knowing if you would ever even see them again.

"Excuse me, Miss," an older gentleman spoke, interrupting Anna's thoughts. He stood before her, dressed in a black suit with silver buttons that traveled its entire length. He was tall, with greying hair and a beard that seemed to add severity to his posture. At first appearance, he was formal and stern, but upon second glance, he looked as if he *could* laugh if the occasion arose.

"Are you waiting for someone?" he inquired; his tone was kind.

"Yes, sir, I am waiting for my aunt." Anna spoke in the sweetest voice she could muster.

"Did she say she would be meeting you here?"

"I am not quite certain, sir, though I do remember her saying something along those lines. But our train was delayed in Hingham for almost a week before our departure here, so she may not have known the exact date of my arrival." Anna paused for a moment, considering her options. "I may need to secure passage to Carpathia if she doesn't arrive soon."

"I see." the man said, not taking his eyes off her. "And who might you be?" he asked.

"Oh, I'm Anna Haddington," Anna replied, her words holding a slight apologetic tone for not introducing herself sooner.

He shook Anna's hand and gave her a slight bow.

"I'm pleased to make your acquaintance, Miss Haddington," he said, his mustache twitching as if trying hard not to smile. "And who is your aunt?"

"Jane Willowbee," Anna replied.

All the color drained from the gentleman's face as the words escaped Anna's lips.

"Jane who?" he choked, his voice sounding strained and forced.

"Willowbee," Anna replied. "Jane Willowbee."

A lady, sitting only a few feet away from Anna, gasped. Another lady in the corner sighed heavily and said, "Oh, the poor thing."

Anna observed the gentleman in confusion. "What is it?" she murmured, her voice breaking. Her face turned ashen white as she awaited the gentleman's response. She was unable to breathe as her heart caught in her throat.

"I'm sorry I must be the one to tell you this ma'am," he spoke quietly, "but your aunt is dead."

Two

"Shall I wait fo ya, sah?" a servant inquired, his voice showing slight alarm.

"No," Prince William Caverly responded, his tone clipped. He took the reins from the servant's outstretched hands and mounted his horse.

He broke the horse into a gallop and rode as quickly as he could from the castle, hoping that there was a way to flee from his problems just as easily. His horse, aching to run, didn't need any more urging. Not until they were well out of sight of Pearlington Palace, did William finally slow her down.

"And he thinks he can tell me what to do!" William yelled angrily. "I'm quite old enough to make my own plans and come and go as I wish!"

But he's your father, his conscience whispered. *You owe him at least a little respect.*

"I don't owe him anything!" he spat. "And don't even start telling me how I owe *anyone* anything. Considering how much Father owes almost everyone he knows, you shouldn't dare even think of telling me such nonsense!"

Pulling on his ho̤ e's reins, William slowed her to a stop. "And here I am carrying on an argument with myself again," he muttered. "Mother always did say I could even argue with a silver candle stick."

At the thought of his mother, sadness filled his being.

Why did she have to die?

He had asked himself that question many times since his mother's death fourteen years ago to the day. He dismounted his horse, Averia, and tied her to a tree. Averia soon began munching on the sweet grass growing nearby. William walked the short distance to the creek and sat down upon a rock, allowing his thoughts to take him far away....

"Happy Birthday, William!" Queen Isabelle spoke softly, reaching out to give her small son a hug. "You are almost a man now!"

At six years old, William hadn't even started thinking of becoming a man yet, but those words had stuck with him and he had tried harder than ever to become the man his mother wanted him to be.

"Are you going to be at my party, Mother?" William had asked. It was to be a grand occasion, with feasting and games and music and gifts. It was enough to make any six-year-old grow wild with delight.

"Yes, my son, I wouldn't miss it for anything in the world." And she had been there, William remembered, propped up with several pillows, reclining on a chair. He remembered watching her there, her face as white as snow. And he knew it had caused her a great deal of pain to be there that night. But she smiled. Through all her pain, she smiled. As far back as William could remember, that smile never left her face. Even up until her death, she had a calm and peaceful countenance. He still wondered how she could have been so peaceful, knowing that any day could have been her last.

He would never forget their last conversation together. Through all the years after her death, he still remembered, though he still did not understand what his mother had tried to tell him.

"William, my son," she told him seriously. "You must repent of your sins."

"What sins, Mama?" He'd tried very hard to be good these past few weeks. He had been very quiet when playing inside and had even offered to help the maid tidy up the nursery. What could he have possibly done wrong?

"You have broken the law."

Isabelle cringed at the way her words sounded, but what else was she supposed to tell him? Raymond had commanded her not to speak about Jesus with William. When she'd questioned him about it, he had shrugged and told her not to worry. *"Religion is like a wall that weak people lean up against. We aren't weak, and we don't need religion."* His words had surprised Isabelle greatly. When had he formed such strong opinions about that matter? She'd never known him to act in such a way before.

But she was no longer afraid of disobeying him. William needed to know about Jesus. He needed to know about the Man who has saved his soul from hell.

William's eyes were full of fright as he looked up into his mother's face. He knew people who broke laws were severely punished.

"Shall I be killed, Mama?" he asked, his eyes shining with tears.

"Yes, son, you deserve to be." And with that, William burst into tears. When his crying had subsided, his mother took him gently by the shoulders. "But, my dear son." Isabelle's soft voice shook with emotion. "Someone offered to take your sins upon Himself and bear the punishment you deserve." Tears rolled unashamedly down his mother's cheeks as she went on. "He is perfect, and He has never sinned or broken any laws, but He was willing to die in *your* place."

William glanced at his mother, astonished. "Who, Mama? Who took my place?"

"His name, my son," answered his mother, "His name is—" She gasped and her voice left her. Composing herself, she tried to speak, but her words only came out a mere rasp.

A maid quickly came in and took him out of the room.

He tried to come back later, but they wouldn't let him in. Throughout the day, he stayed by his mother's door, but he never had the opportunity to speak with her again. He went to bed that night with a heavy heart.

"I should be happy," he told himself. "I'm not going to be killed. But it's not fair someone perfect should die in my place."

Why would he do that for me? *Who* would do that for me? Who is he? And into the night, even in his dreams, one could hear the child murmur, *who is he? Who is he?*

The next morning, he awoke to crying and weeping like he had never heard before.

He quickly ran to his mother's room. The door was open; she must be all right. He slowly went to his mother's bedside. She was so white and still. He reached out a hand to touch hers. It was cold. And then the realization hit him: She was gone. His precious mother, whom he had loved, whom he *did* love, was gone. Panic seized him as he realized she had not told him who had taken his punishment.

"Who is he, Mama?" he cried loudly. "Who is he?"

Someone came into the room and tried to lead him away, but he clung to his mother's hand, not willing to let go.

"Who is he, Mama?" he sobbed. He heard his father's footsteps behind him, but he didn't turn around. William sunk onto his knees and sobbed uncontrollably, the entire time murmuring, "Who is he? Who is he?"

"Take him away," he heard his father say behind him, his tone strained and broken. "Keep him in his room until I give word otherwise."

It was then that he had first noticed the lack of compassion that his father began to bestow. His wife's death had changed him, and not for the better. But had death ever changed anyone for the better? William glanced up at the mountains stretching far into the deep blue sky and knew it had. It had changed *him*. That unknown person who took his place in death had changed everything for him. He had taken William's sins upon himself, and suffered the punishment he deserved. William wiped at the tears rolling unchecked down his cheeks.

"Who was he?" he spoke into the wind. "He died in my place. And I never even got the chance to thank him."

And resting his head against his folded arms, he wept.

There were no tears from Anna. They just wouldn't come.

She couldn't tell much of what happened over the next few minutes. But she was aware of being taken somewhere, in a room off to the side of the ticket office. The room smelled musty, as if it had not been used in months.

She sat down in the corner of the small room and stayed there. She was frozen, numb. Her mind couldn't grasp the news she had just been told. A pleasant-faced lady came into the room and set a tray of food upon the bed, but Anna didn't move. She only hugged her knees close to her body, willing this to just be a dream.

At some point she fell asleep, the tray of food untouched.

When Anna awoke, night had already fallen. A slight chill ran about the room, but she was too full of grief to worry about it.

It was then that Anna wept. Sobs shook her slight frame as she cried for her aunt, the death that had taken her from this earth, and for her siblings. The month she had been away from them had already began to seem like a lifetime.

But Anna didn't weep for long. She had been taught to face trials courageously, and though that was the furthest thing she felt at the moment, she decided to put what her father and mother had taught her into action. She slowly stood, unaware of her surroundings. She felt around, willing her hands to be her eyes.

Feeling to her right, her hand bumped against something soft. The bed.

She slowly made her way to the end of the room.

Her fingers scratched against what felt like the smooth top of a table. There. A box. Trembling fingers closed around a box of matches and her hand bumped slightly against the coldness of a lantern. She struck a match and held it to the wick. The light shone throughout the room.

In the corner was a bed, and beside the bed stood a small wooden table.

She made her way across the room to her brown valise and withdrew her most prized possession: her Bible.

She ran her fingers over the black leather cover and held it tightly to her chest. Making her way back to the table at the front of the room, she set the lantern upon it, pulled out a chair and sat down. She gently placed her Bible beside her, opened it, and began to read:

"But I would not have you to be ignorant, brethren, concerning them which are asleep, that ye sorrow not, even as others which have no hope.
For if we believe that Jesus died and rose again, even so them also which sleep in Jesus will God bring with Him.
For this we say unto you by the word of the Lord, that we which are alive and remain unto

*the coming of the Lord shall not prevent them
which are asleep.
For the Lord Himself shall descend from heaven
with a shout, with the voice of the archangel,
and with the trump of God: and the dead in
Christ shall rise first:
Then we which are alive and remain shall be
caught up together with them in the clouds, to
meet the Lord in the air: and so shall we ever be
with the Lord.
Wherefore comfort one another with these
words."*

A quiet peace began to settle over Anna. Aunt Jane was saved. She spoken to father often in her letters about God and how He had changed her life.

The quiet peace turned into a calm reassurance as she continued to read another passage:

"For His anger endureth but a moment; in His favor is life: weeping may endure for a night, but joy cometh in the morning."

She left her Bible upon the table and blew out the lantern. She slipped off her black boots and placed them by the wall. Sliding under the heavy blanket, she was at once thankful for its warmth.

With a prayer upon her lips, she drifted off to sleep.

The next morning, the sun was shining brightly. Despite the disturbing news the day before, Anna woke up feeling strangely at peace.

She stepped outside and breathed deeply of the crisp morning air.

A few feet away stood the ticket station. She walked up the flight of steps, clasping tightly to her valise, and opened the door. As soon as she stepped inside, she was greeted by a flood of warmth and the strong smell of coffee. There were only a few people in the station and none of them looked familiar to her. At the sound of the door opening, everyone turned and looked at Anna.

"The poor thing," she heard someone murmur.

"And she's so young," another whispered.

"Likely doesn't have a cent to her name," scoffed a gentleman behind the counter.

Anna blushed as she looked around for the gentleman who had helped her the night before.

"Um, pardon me for asking, but do you happen to know where I can find the gentleman who was here last night?" Anna asked hesitantly.

"What do you want with that stingy landlord?" asked a heavy-set lady in the corner of the room.

Anna was taken aback by the woman's gruffness. "I wanted to thank him for his kindness to me last night," she responded, her tone a bit abrupt.

She was greeted by blank stares from all around.

"Thank him?" the lady's voice was edged with surprise.

"Thank him?" the gentleman scoffed. "Little lady," he replied, "that old man doesn't deserve a hint of thanks, in fact, the only thanks he ever deserved was when...wait, he didn't deserve that thanks either!"

The room erupted into laughter.

"I'm sorry to have bothered you," Anna said quietly. She stepped outside and briskly walked away from the ticket station. She couldn't help but feel sorry for the poor man, who seemed to have few friends left in the world.

He hadn't seemed so grouchy to *her*.

She wished she could speak with him again. She could have told him about a friend who would never leave or forsake him.

She could only hope and pray he already knew about that Friend, or perhaps he was friends with Him already. Leaving the crowded boat dock, she paid careful attention to her surroundings.

She must find work, or at least a place to work in exchange for room and board. But as she walked in and out of the many shops, she began to grow discouraged.

She couldn't grow weary. She *had* to persevere. God had a plan for her arrival here. She just needed to discover it.

After another hour of searching, the sun's heat was pouring down upon the town, and Anna had grown weak from lack of food and water. She decided to ask to spend the night in one of the neighbors' homes, or at least get a drink of water and a wholesome meal.

After walking for another hour, she was convinced she had taken the road leading out of town.

Her head had begun to grow faint and her heart beat quickly. Her legs buckled underneath her as she fell towards the ground.

Even amidst her fading surroundings, a comforting verse filled her mind,

> *"The Lord is their strength, and He is the saving strength of His anointed."*

"Lord, please be my strength!" Anna cried.
Then the world went black.

Three

"Is there anything else you might be needing?" William politely asked his grandmother.

They were in the palace library, having just taken their afternoon tea. William had read aloud to his grandmother while she ate, knowing she enjoyed it very much. With it being her birthday and all, he figured he could do her at least that small of a favor. He set the volume upon a low table, having just finished the chapter.

"Some more knitting needles, perhaps," she answered, her voice sounding tired and strained. "And some more of the bright blue yarn your father likes so much."

William didn't know where his grandmother had gotten the idea that his father liked the blue yarn. In fact, his father utterly detested blue, but William was not about to tell his grandmother that.

He didn't linger at the palace for very long; the day was wasting away.

Making his way outside, he took his horse, Averia, from a servant and quickly mounted.

As he rode towards the town, he thought of his birthday coming up soon.

He was turning twenty-one, and the thought both frightened and excited him. There was a great deal of responsibility falling upon his shoulders. Someday, he would be king of Pearlington Palace and all the land beneath it.

But as he continued on his way, all thoughts of kingship soon vanished from his mind. Not far ahead of him, a figure lay motionless on the ground. Beside the figure stood a man, but William was too far away to see his face.

William gently tapped Averia with his whip, breaking her into a quick trot. They soon came upon them. "Can I be of any assistance?" William offered, his face clearly showing concern.

"Yes, do you—" the man stopped as he turned toward him. "I – I meant, no, Your Majesty! Sorry to bother you, sir!"

William dismounted his horse and quickly closed the distance between them. It was then that he noticed that the figure lying on the ground was a young woman. "I would like to help," William said firmly.

The man looked at him with surprise. "She needs some water. She seems to have fainted; from what, I am not yet certain."

William went to his horse, withdrew the water he had brought, and handed it to the man. A soft moan escaped the girl's lips as the man bent down and gently lifted her head from the ground.

"Here," he commanded. "You need to drink this."

She slowly drank some of the cool liquid. Her eyes fluttered open and filled with confusion as she tried to comprehend what was happening.

The man beside her spoke first. "I'm Johnathan Clark, ma'am. We're here to help you. Can you think back as to what happened?"

The young lady struggled to stand up. Johnathan reached out a caring hand to steady her. He helped her to a nearby tree, and she sat down, leaning against it for support.

"Thank you kindly for your help," she said gratefully, her voice still slightly weak.

Johnathan nodded. "You're very welcome, Miss."

They were patient as they waited for her story.

"I'm Anna," she responded to their questioning stares. "I arrived here from France yesterday to live with my aunt."

Anna's story unfolded upon listening ears, and not until she had told them everything did they finally speak.

"And you have nowhere to go?" William spoke to her for the first time.

Anna turned toward him. "I could go back home," she said doubtfully. "But I would need to work for a while to get enough money for passage."

Johnathan handed her the water again and she drank deeply.

"What you need is a wholesome meal and a good night's rest," Johnathan said with authority. "I'm just passing through, or my wife and I wouldn't hesitate in offering our house to you."

"You are very kind, sir," Anna said genuinely. "I could try to sleep at the station again." The very thought of going back there made her cringe.

"Nonsense!" William burst out. "You shall do no such thing. Not if I can help it."

He left the tree and went to his horse. Withdrawing his money bag, he took out several coins. He came back and placed them in Anna's hand.

"Oh, sir, I cannot thank you enough for your generosity!"

"That should be enough for several days' board, including meals," William said.

Anna's eyes filled with gratitude as she thanked him again.

"I can recommend a few places that might be of interest to you," William suggested.

Anna nodded. "I would be most grateful."

"I am on my way through town now," said Johnathan. "So, I shall walk with you there."

"So am I," William added. "You shall have two escorts!"

When Johnathan helped Anna onto his horse, the three set off towards the town.

It took them a few minutes to reach the town, but William and Johnathan kept the conversation flowing. It seemed as if time almost escaped them.

Soon, they arrived in front of a very well-kept boarding house.

"I hear Tilly, the owner of this boarding house, happens to be one of the best cooks around," William commented as they made their way up a flight of steps.

They helped Anna with her luggage and made sure she was settled before they left.

"Thank you again for everything," Anna said gratefully.

They went their separate ways, William going into town and Johnathan continuing his journey homeward.

Thank You, Lord, for the people you put in our lives, Anna thought, as she made her way to her room. *If they had not found me today, I might not have been here tomorrow.*

Anna soon heard the call for dinner, and, being as hungry as she was, she needed no second bidding. She was so famished she could have eaten *anything.* Anna quickly finished the steaming bowl of vegetable stew set before her. She had never tasted anything so delightful. Thick slices of bread with rich pats of butter, and pastries for dessert, made Anna feel as if she had just eaten a feast.

The rest of the boarding house guests kept up a lively conversation, but Anna stayed quiet and listened intently, feeling rather out of place, though she didn't know why.

Once she had finished her meal, Anna left for her room.

Crossing the room to where her valise sat, she carefully withdrew her Bible. Setting it on a small table next to the window, she sat down upon the bed, taking time to observe her room.

The room was painted the color of freshly churned butter, the trim a lovely shade of pink.

The bed frame was made of the darkest wood she had ever seen and was smooth to the touch. In the corner of the room stood a wash basin and pitcher, both of which were hand-painted with tiny red rosebuds and even smaller leaves of bright green.

Anna put what few clothes she had into the drawers standing next to the bed.

Just as she was about to change into a clean set of clothes, there was a knock at her door. Anna opened it with slight apprehension.

"I was told you might be wantin' to take a bath, Miss," a maid spoke, not looking Anna in the eye.

"Yes, thank you." Anna replied, a small smile lifting the corners of her mouth. "A bath does indeed sound delightful."

After the maid finished hauling the heated water and pouring it into the washtub, she left Anna in peace.

The water had never felt so good, and Anna was delighted with the luxury. Not knowing how long she should take, she did not linger. She dressed in a simple evening gown and decided to rest for a while, but Anna was so tired from the last few days that she instead drifted into a deep sleep.

When she awoke, the sun was shining brightly through the window, its rays dancing about the room in a merry fashion as if to say 'Wake up! It's morning!'

But Anna did not notice the light, nor was her heart in such a merry state.

What was she going to do? Where would she go? She felt for the first time in her life that the Lord had forsaken her. It felt as if He had left her all alone to decide what to do next.

Anna had just finished dressing when a slight knock upon her door startled her. She opened the door cautiously, but smiled when she noticed the maid from the night before. "Thers' a gentleman askin' to see ya, Miss. He be waitin' in the drawin' room."

Anna thanked her kindly and went directly downstairs. She walked down the narrow hall, passing the kitchen on her way. The aroma of freshly baked bread wafted through the house, reminding Anna of home. When she stepped into the drawing room, her eyes immediately rested upon William. He was standing before the window, his back turned away from her as he stared out into the street.

At the sound of her footsteps, William spun around. "Miss Anna, how are you?" Without waiting for an answer, he hurried on. "I trust you had an excellent dinner last evening?"

"I did, thank you. It was the best meal I have had in a long while. I cannot thank you enough for your kindness."

William smiled. "I'm just glad I came along when I did. What do you plan to do now?" he asked, concern showing in his voice.

Anna was curious as to why he had come to see her again so soon; whatever it was, he wasn't getting to the point very quickly.

"I suppose I should continue to look for employment," she answered politely.

"Excellent," said William with a smile. "I happen to know my head housekeeper is looking to hire a scullery maid."

Ah, so that was it. He had come to offer her a working position. Looking at his attire, he lived, no doubt, in a very wealthy family. But if that were the case, then why was he concerned about the head housekeeper's affairs? Or about *hers* for that matter.

"A scullery maid?" she echoed.

"Yes." His face colored slightly.

Anna thought about his offer for a moment, but decided it was too important of a decision to make alone.

"I may be inclined to accept, but if you would only be so kind as to wait a bit longer for my answer, I would be most grateful."

"You would?" he asked. "Wonderful! Yes, take as long as you need. I shall send a carriage for you in about a week. If you decide to decline my offer, then just send the carriage right back."

"Thank you very much. I am sure that shall be plenty of time."

"Good day, then," William replied, giving her a slight bow.

As Anna watched his retreating figure, a scripture filled her mind.

"The Lord preserveth all them that love Him...."

Shame and remorse quickly filled her soul.

Why did she have such a hard time trusting in God? He had never let her down before, so why must she doubt Him the second she face a trial? The Lord had graciously saved her from possible death and had now shown that He was continuing to look after her. Why must she continue to doubt His loving care and guidance?

The day passed quickly for Anna, and as she prepared for bed that evening, she took special attention in her attitude toward the Lord. After reading a few chapters in Psalms, she knelt by her bedside to pray.

"Thank You, Lord, for not forsaking me, even when I deserve to be forsaken. Thank You for providing for my every need. Please fill me with Your wisdom and help me to trust You and to not doubt You. Please make it clear if I should work for William's family. Please forgive me when I sin against You. Thank You that, through our sufferings, we can still

have the reassurance that You shall never leave us, nor forsake us...."

Anna's prayer continued late into the night.

The reassurance that the Lord would never leave her brought her much comfort and joy.

Little did she know, she would soon need Him more than she ever had before.

Four

"You did *what*?" King Raymond yelled in a fit of rage.

"She needed help, Father!" William defended himself. "She needed work and a place to stay."

Raymond Caverly's face was red with fury. "We don't help the poor," he spat. "They help *us!*"

William glared at his father and obstinately continued, "She is a hard worker, Father. I am sure she will be a great deal of help to the servants."

But even as he said this, William knew he had made an awful mistake. *Why did I offer her this position? And why of all things did I wait until the end of the week to tell Father?*

Anna would be here any minute. He had no time to take back his offer.

William suddenly hoped with all his might she would decline his proposition and send the carriage back empty.

William's attention was brought back to the moment as his father began speaking again.

"That's fine," Raymond suddenly announced, a disquieting gleam in his eyes. "I should not have reacted so quickly. Let her come."

He gave William a fatherly pat on the shoulder and turned to leave the library. But William's heart sank at the words. What had changed the king's mind so quickly? He could only guess, and he grew sick at the thought.

What have I done? William murmured inwardly, a heavy weight sinking to the pit of his stomach. *What have I done?*

The week flew by so quickly for Anna that she hardly had time to think. She had many opportunities to help a widow staying in the room next to hers. With her three rowdy children, Anna was kept very busy indeed.

She told them Bible stories and sang to them while their mother was away looking for employment. She also made sure the children were fed and put to bed each night their mother came home late.

One evening as she was dressing three-year-old Michael, she heard his older sister Ada crying softly in her bed. Anna tucked Michael into his bed of blankets on the floor, sang him a quiet lullaby, and made sure baby Charity was fast asleep in her cradle before coming to Ada's bedside.

"What's the matter, Ada?" she asked tenderly. Sitting down on the bed, she tucked a strand of Ada's hair behind her ear.

"What if something happens to my mama?" Ada sobbed quietly. "I already lost my papa, how can I bear to lose Mama, too?"

Anna gently placed Ada in her lap and waited until her tears had subsided. "The Lord has told us in His Word that we are His children and nothing can ever change that," Anna began, "He has told us we are not to worry and be anxious about tomorrow and the things that *could* happen, because He is already in the future and knows *all* things. And your papa is gone away from you only a short while, for someday you shall all be together again and live in heaven with him for eternity!"

Ada looked up at Anna, the light of peace shining in her eight-year-old face. "Mama told us Jesus is a

Father to the Fatherless, so that makes Him your Father too, doesn't it?"

Anna nodded, tears glistening in her eyes.

"So that makes us sisters!" Ada exclaimed, throwing her hands around Anna's waist and hugging her tightly.

Anna nodded, a smile playing about her lips. "Yes, dear one," she replied, kissing the top of Ada's flaxen curls. "Sisters in Christ."

Anna's week drew quickly to a close, and the talk with Ada and the news that Ada's mother had found work had been the highlight of her stay.

"I can't thank you enough!" Ada's mother had told her, her eyes shining with emotion. "Thanks to you, I have been able to find a job mending clothes for a wealthy family in town!"

Anna was very glad to be of help, and she had a hard time telling the children goodbye the night before her departure. But, she managed it somehow, and before she knew it, she found herself preparing for her last night at the boarding house.

The pleasant sound of chirping birds woke Anna the next morning.

She dressed slowly, choosing her apparel carefully, though with her limited supply, there wasn't much to choose from.

She decided on a light blue calico print. Pinning her long brown hair back into a loose bun, she glanced out the window and marveled at how the week had flown by.

There was a knock at her door just as she finished her hair, and laying aside her brush, she went quickly to answer it.

"Good morning!" said a pleasant-faced woman, who looked to be in her mid-forties. Her blonde hair was pulled back in a tight bun and she was dressed in a plain brown dress with a crisp white apron.

"I'm Tilly, the owner of this boarding house," she said, a bit grandly.

"And I'm Anna," she replied.

The lady smiled. "I have been visiting my sister who just had her tenth child, bless her soul, so I am here to offer my deep regrets that I have been away, and to make sure my daughter has taken care of your every need."

Anna smiled gratefully. "She has been most kind, I assure you. And I am leaving today, so I shouldn't be any more trouble to you."

The lady looked almost relieved, and replied, "Very well. Oh, breakfast shall be ready at an eight till quarter." She held up her hand. "I mean, a quarter till eight!" She laughed awkwardly and began to knock on the next row of doors.

"Thank you," Anna answered, "I shall be there." But the lady didn't hear, as she had already began speaking to the next boarder.

Anna closed the door softly and sat down at the small table, deciding to read until breakfast.

"And, behold, a certain lawyer stood up, and tempted Him, saying, Master, what shall I do to inherit eternal life?

He said unto him, what is written in the law? How readest thou?

And he answering said, thou shalt love the Lord thy God with all thy heart, and with all thy soul, and with all thy strength, and with all thy mind; and thy neighbor as thyself.

And He said unto him, thou hast answered right: this do, and thou shalt live.

But he, willing to justify himself, said unto Jesus, and who is my neighbor?

And Jesus answering said, A certain man went down from Jerusalem to Jericho, and fell among thieves, which stripped him of his raiment, and wounded him, and departed, leaving him half dead.

And by chance there came down a certain priest that way: and when he saw him, he passed by on the other side.

And likewise a Levite, when he was at the place, came and looked on him, and passed by on the other side.

But a certain Samaritan, as he journeyed, came where he was: and when he saw him, he had compassion on him,

And went to him, and bound up his wounds, pouring in oil and wine, and set him on his own beast, and brought him to an inn, and took care of him.

And on the morrow when he departed, he took out two pence, and gave them to the host, and said unto him, take care of him; and whatsoever thou spendest more, when I come again, I will repay thee.

Which now of these three, thinkest thou, was neighbor unto him that fell among the thieves?

And he said, He that shewed mercy on him.

Then said Jesus unto him, Go, and do thou likewise."

A smile lifted the corners of Anna's mouth as she thought about the passage she'd just read. The gentlemen last week were *her* Samaritans. They obeyed Jesus and went and did likewise. She wondered if they knew about Jesus and what He did for them.

Anna did find it slightly strange that she had seen no copies of the Bible since her arrival here. And upon thinking about it, she hadn't seen any churches either.

Anna glanced at the sun and decided she should leave now for the dining room. She remembered the fuss her mother had always made about being on time. *'It shows we care about our host and the time they have put into everything,'* her mother's words came back to her. *It is polite,* Anna reasoned.

Making sure to close the door behind her, she made her way to the dining room. The smell of fresh biscuits greeted her even before they could be seen. She smiled at the guests already seated and gracefully took her seat.

Soon their breakfast was served, consisting of fluffy buttermilk biscuits, eggs, bacon and gravy. A platter filled with oranges, strawberries and lightly-whipped cream also graced the table.

If there was one thing Anna had learned during her stay, it was that they never lacked for food.

Anna quietly bowed her head and thanked the Lord for the bountiful food he had bestowed upon her and for providing for her needs yet again.

She was almost done eating when Tilly came into the dining room, curiosity showing visibly on her face. "A carriage has arrived for you, Miss Haddington," she spoke, her voice filled with surprise.

Anna glanced her way. "Please tell them I shall be just a moment."

She left the table and went up to her room, grabbed her valise—which she had packed the night before—and made her way down the flight of stairs. As she neared the door, she could hear several voices talking excitedly. People soon clustered all around her, talking in rapid tones.

"Goodbye, M'lady." A woman in a bright yellow dress curtsied.

A gentleman bowed. "It's been a pleasure making your acquaintance, Miss."

"Your presence has added such a bright spot at our breakfast table!" a young lady said, fluttering her eyelashes.

Anna looked at them in surprise. She did her best to smile, but found the whole situation quite startling.

Tilly met her at the door with a smile. "I feel so honored having you at my boarding house!" she said warmly, giving Anna a hug.

"Don't ever forget me!" she heard someone squeal behind her as the door closed shut on the bewildering scene.

Anna's brow furrowed in confusion. It was impossible to forget someone whom you've never even met!

But the sight that greeted Anna's eyes did little to ease the confusion from her mind.

"I don't believe I have ever seen anything so elegant!" Anna gasped.

Before her stood the most magnificent horse and carriage she had ever seen. The carriage was pure white and trimmed with gold, sparkling in the sunlight. The transport was drawn by two rich, ebony black horses; beauties, the noblest steeds Anna had ever laid eyes on.

A man came forward and gave her a deep bow. "It is my sincere pleasure to serve you today, Miss," he said, in a thick French accent.

He took Anna's luggage and another man stood by the carriage to help her in.

"*Merci*, sir," Anna said, thanking him in French. She sat upon the lush, red velvet seats and looked around, a bit unsettled.

A man sat in the seat across from Anna. He looked very solemn, which didn't ease Anna's feeling of uncertainty much. He was dressed in a white suit with shiny black buttons that traveled the entire length.

She smiled at the man, but he only nodded in response. "I am afraid there has been a terrible mistake," Anna said hesitantly.

"Oh, trust me," the man said, his lips curling into a malicious smile, "this is no mistake."

Anna glanced out the window and wondered if she should turn back. But no, she refused to retreat so quickly.

She felt a slight peace steal its way over her heart as she thought of the scripture her father had always quoted when things seemed uncertain,

"For I know the thoughts that I think toward you, saith the Lord, thoughts of peace and not of evil, to give you an expected end."

The Lord has my future already planned for me, Anna thought to herself. *Why must I continue to doubt His guidance? He has promised to take care*

of me and to never leave nor forsake me. Why do I feel such uncertainty about the future? If these are trials that You are sending my way, then, Lord, help me to not come out broken, but refined.

Her mother's words came back to her:

'Trials are God's way of showing us He's still there, allowing us to call upon Him for help. God knows our every weakness and, sometimes, He sends trials our way to strengthen us. Other times, He wants us to be a light and a witness to the perishing, and the perishing aren't usually in the most comfortable of situations, but He sends us to them to be a witness. But we must trust, we must always trust in the Lord, even when His plans may seem a bit unsettling, we must trust....''

They traveled for several minutes until suddenly a shout from nearby brought Anna back to the present.

"Whoa there, boys!" the driver yelled.

They pulled to a not-so-gentle stop and the man across from Anna alighted from the carriage and stepped to the side to assist her. As Anna stepped down to the ground, she looked around in awe. Before her towered the most spectacular palace she had ever seen.

"Come this way, Miss." The man in the white suit motioned for her to follow him. Anna followed submissively, even though she longed to turn back. She felt very small as she looked up at the giant palace. The pillars of the magnificent dwelling stretched far into the bright blue sky.

"Let down the drawbridge!" a man yelled in the distance.

It was then that Anna noticed the enormous wooden bridge towering over them. With a shuddering rumble, the bridge began to lower into place.

Anna watched as the drawbridge lowered across the moat filled with greenish-brown water. She wondered what lay beyond its murky depths. Her body trembled, more from the misgivings of her situation than from the slight breeze. She followed the man across the bridge, making sure to stay away from the edge, but she couldn't resist one look into the deep brown waters.

Two men were awaiting her arrival and opened an enormous iron gate. Anna walked through, apprehension growing with her every step. And every step brought her closer to the mystery that lay beyond the palace walls.

Five

 William glanced out of the palace window and his heart sank.

She came. After all that hoping, she had actually come.

He wished there was something he could do. But he knew if he tried to interfere now, it wouldn't go well for him *or* Anna.

After letting his father know that he had offered Anna a position, William had quickly made himself absent. *I could have gone and met the carriage.* William muttered to himself, only thinking of it at this very moment.

But his father had no doubt been watching William's every move. He wouldn't have gotten past the first gate without being commanded to return. And when one didn't obey the commands of the king... William shuddered at the recollection. Things didn't go well for them.

He pulled on a light jacket and descended the steps, buttoning it as he went. Usually, he would have been annoyed at the many buttons, but now... now, he wished there were a thousand. Anything than to have to go and confront this situation.

He met his father at the door and knew he had been waiting for him.

"Hurry!" the king yelled impatiently. He stood, rubbing his hands together in great excitement, a sly smile playing about his lips.

"You don't really want to do this, Father," William said carefully, in a last attempt to deter his plans.

"Oh, yes, I do," Raymond replied with a smile. He turned toward a servant standing guard by the door. "Open that door, you scoundrel!"

The man jerked upright and quickly did as he was told.

Raymond walked briskly out the door, his head held high in the air.

William followed behind him, wishing he were a thousand miles away.

"My dear madam!" the king said, smiling at Anna. Anna looked at William, alarm and confusion clearly showing upon her face, but William looked away.

It was then that William noticed the carriage that had been sent to bring Anna here. It was the king's carriage. No doubt sent by King Raymond himself. How could she refuse when the king's carriage was right at her doorstep? Raymond was making every possible attempt to keep her here. But why?

If only she had refused my offer, William thought. *If only she turned back, if only...* but William could no longer think of the things that *could* happen. She was here and she could no longer turn back; his father would make sure of that.

But Anna was speaking, and he did his best to listen.

"Your Majesty!" Anna spoke with reverence. She lowered her head in respect and would have bowed if the king had not restrained her.

"Now, none of that!" he commanded, his tone edged with slight impatience.

William squeezed his hands into tight fists. Relaxing them, he let them fall limp by his side. "I trust your stay at the boarding house was satisfactory?"

Anna stared at him uncertainly. "Yes, thank you, it was. And is this where I shall be working?"

William couldn't answer, so he merely nodded.

The king spoke for him, "Yes, yes, my dear! And you shall not regret it, I will assure you of that."

Anna glanced at William and then back at the king, no doubt still terribly confused.

"Come this way, my dear," the king told her. He led her to the palace library, where the documents were to be signed.

Anna looked around in astonishment. Finery and worldly possessions could not control her, but books could. The exclamation of delight Anna showed as they walked through the doors into the library, gave the king a weakness he would soon take advantage of.

Anna had never seen so many books before, and she was quite amazed by them all. This was one of the largest rooms in the palace. Bookcases lined the walls and wrapped around most of the room. Chairs were placed here and there, looking comfortable and inviting. A giant table sat in the center of the room on a lush carpet of velvet, with several chairs fixed around it. A giant window ran along the whole length of the front wall, letting one see the palace garden and the forest beyond the castle. The window let much light into the library, making the table and chairs almost seem as if they were sparkling. And the strong smell of leather couldn't go unnoticed.

William wished she hadn't shown so much interest.

"Come right this way." The king stepped to the side, letting Anna pass him.

He motioned to a chair in front of the table and she sat down. He walked behind the table and stood, looking down at her, as if inspecting her to make sure she was acceptable. When he was satisfied with what he saw, he made a sweeping motion with his hand toward the entire room and spoke in his deep voice. "You'll be pleased to learn that all our servants receive unlimited access to the library on their breaks."

William looked at his father, astonished. When had he made *that* rule? And—on their *breaks*? As far as William knew, the only 'breaks' the servants got were the ones from being worked too hard. But William, once again, remained quiet.

"Just sign this and your life shall be changed forever," the king said, smiling down at Anna.

Well, thought William, *that must be the first true thing he has said since her arrival.*

Anna took the paper from him hesitantly, then gave the paper her full attention and began to read.

The king must not have expected Anna to read the entire document, for soon, he grew impatient, much to William's delight. King Raymond shifted from one leg to another, watching her, eagerly waiting for her to finish. When she finished reading, she looked at William, and then at the king.

"Well?" Raymond asked, looking at her, trying very hard not to show his impatience.

Anna spoke clearly and without hesitation, "I do not make such important decisions without consulting my Father first. I hope you understand," she added kindly.

Anna was stalling for more time, but she couldn't think of any other tactic. She was beginning to feel very uneasy about all this.

The king stared at her in shock. "Your what?" he asked incredulously.

"My Father," she replied definitively.

"But-but your father is dead," he stammered.

Anna wondered where he had gathered that information. *He must have heard it from William,* she concluded.

"My Heavenly Father," Anna tried to explain, hoping he would understand.

"I see," the king said slowly. "Well, since I am a very loving and patient man... I shall give you five minutes!" He smiled at himself, as if proud of his generosity.

Anna was shocked; that wasn't exactly what she had in mind. But five minutes was better than nothing at all, and so she accepted.

William left with his father. If there's a God out there at all, then he would save Anna from making this decision. No loving God would allow such a thing to happen.

If You allow Anna to be saved from the wretched life my father must have in mind, if You, somehow, make her refuse to sign that paper and see her safely back to her home, then I might consider believing in You.

Strangely, a sense of peace began to creep into his body. God would take him up on his offer... wouldn't He?

Anna looked around the large library, feeling very small indeed. She wondered if she was making a very big mistake.

Dear Father in heaven, she prayed. *I need Your help so very badly. You know all that has been happening the last few weeks. You know I lost my dear father and Auntie and now must make this important decision. Please give me peace about this decision I must make, please show me the right way to go. Please help me not to make a decision I will regret. Please, Lord, help me to make a decision that would be honoring not only to my father and mother, but also to You. I want to honor You, Lord, and do what is right in Your sight. Please help to make my decision clear and show me the right way to go. In Your holy name I pray, Amen.*

Six

The king walked back into the room. "Well?" he questioned.

Anna confidently answered, "I accept."

The king relaxed, a smile lighting up his countenance. "Good, very good. Just sign this," he handed her a single piece of parchment.

William's legs threatened to buckle underneath him and his heart grew hard. He had prayed and God hadn't listened.

Anna took the pen in her slender hand and began to sign.

William couldn't stay silent any longer; it was time to take matters into his own hands. "Don't sign that paper!" he yelled. His voice rang out in the quiet room.

Anna stood up quickly, so alarmed by the outburst that she almost knocked over her chair.

"What is the meaning of this?" the king yelled, glaring at William. His son's outburst had startled him, and he most certainly wasn't going to allow any interference.

William was silent, almost as shocked at himself as his father was. He couldn't find his tongue, so his father found it for him. "Please excuse my son," Raymond apologized, not taking his eyes off William's face. "He has been mentally ill since his dear mother died. What would your mother think, my son?" the king said, a half smile upon his lips. He knew only too well what chord to strike.

William glanced at Anna, whose face had turned from alarm to pity. He turned towards his father, who was staring back at him with a disparaging look he had long become accustomed to. William had seen enough. He spun quickly on his heel and exited the library. When he returned to his room, he pounded the wall in anger. He dropped onto his bed, chest heaving. Someday, his father was going to reap what he sowed, and William would personally see to it.

"Wonderful!" the king said with a smile. "James will show you to your room and you shall start tomorrow morning."

"Thank you, Your Majesty," Anna replied respectfully.

"Oh, it was all my pleasure, dear, my *sincere* pleasure."

Anna was not shown to a room. Instead, she was given a woven mat which was to serve as her bed. She looked up in surprise as James handed it to her, but said nothing.

"You shall report to Betty, the head kitchen maid, for each of your duties," he instructed, showing her to the kitchen. Anna nodded mutely. The kitchen was much larger than she had imagined. She placed her mat in the corner, and, feeling quite tired, she drifted off to sleep.

The next morning, she awoke early. After getting herself ready to go on with her day, she donned an apron and began to wash the kitchen floor, which had been neglected for quite some time.

A dark-skinned lady walked into the kitchen, her disposition rather strict. Behind her followed a young girl around eleven or twelve, Anna guessed.

The lady began instructing the younger girl on how to properly make bubble and squeak. The recipe wasn't difficult, and it was the king's favorite.

The potatoes and cabbage, mixed with a portion of bacon and just the right amount of seasonings, made for a perfect supper.

"No!" the lady burst out. "Not like that!" She took the pile of cabbage and dumped it into a nearby bowl.

The young girl let out a small groan and her shoulders slumped. "I'm sorry, Mrs. Betty," answered the girl, her voice filled with tears.

So *that* was Betty.

Anna coughed somewhat loudly, trying to get Mrs. Betty's attention off the young girl. Betty turned around sharply, clearly upset about being disturbed. It was then that the young girl by the stove turned around as well, and Anna got a good look at her for the first time. Her skin was the same dark brown color as Betty's with eyes that nearly matched her tone.

Betty walked up to Anna, and the closer she got, the shorter Anna realized Betty was; she barely came up to Anna's shoulder, but that didn't stop her from being the boss. Betty came up so close that Anna began to feel a bit uneasy.

She looked Anna up and down slowly. "You's wasted too much of the day already," she began. Anna didn't bother telling her she had been ready and working before the sun had come up. "You ever had any *real* experience in the kitchen?" she snapped.

"Yes, ma'am," Anna replied, trying her best to keep from giving Betty a piece of her mind.

"How abou' washin' clothes?"

Anna replied that she had. Anna thought Betty had finished, but she had only just begun.

"You are ta assist us in keepin' the utensils clean and you'll be washin' every dish that comes into this kitchen. You'll provide hot water for the scullery, kitchen tasks and household. You'll be keepin' the scullery clean by clearin' away meat and vegetable scraps, by scrubbing work tables and sweeping the floors. You will *not* clean the fine china, stemware, crystal or plate silver; these are cleaned by housemaids and footmen. You are responsible for lightin' the fires in the kitchen stove and supplyin' hot water for tea and washin'. You are *not* ta eat in the servants' dining hall, but in the kitchen so tha' you can keep an eye on the food bein' prepared.

After meals, you'll see ta cleanin' and scouring the floors, stoves, sinks, pots and dishes. Your position as a scullery maid is not, of course, one of high rank. But if you's fortunate enough, you may soon learn enough ta be of considerable service in fittin' ya'self for a more responsible place. But ya ain't go'anna get ta that place by bein' lazy!" She paused, catching her breath. "Do I be makin' myself clear?"

Anna's head was spinning, but she found her voice. "Yes, ma'am," she answered weakly, "I think so."

Betty studied Anna and raised her eyebrows. "You *think* so?"

"Yes, ma'am. There was a lot to grasp, but I think I got most of it," Anna said truthfully. "And anything I didn't get I shall learn soon enough, I'm sure."

Betty seemed slightly taken aback by her truthful and direct answer, but tried to mask her surprise. The young girl by the stove gazed at Anna, her eyes wide with curiosity.

"Very well," said Betty. "Your first task shall be to wash this load of dishes." She led Anna over to a corner of the kitchen where a pile of dirty dishes stood, stretching at least four feet high. Anna started washing them straightaway without complaint, much to Betty's curiosity. Seeing that Anna was going to be busy with her task for a while, Betty went back to the not-so-enjoyable instruction of her young charge. "Now, Lilly," she told the young girl, "Let's try this again. And get it right this time!"

Anna began to hum softly as she worked, making her washing more enjoyable. Before she knew it, she had washed every dish. She dried her hands on her apron, noticing they were already red and shriveled.

"They'll get used to it," Lilly told her from her spot by the fire. It was the first time Lilly had spoken to her since her arrival in the kitchen, the reason being that Betty had just stepped out of the room.

"I must have been away from my duties for far too long!" Anna laughed.

"I'm Lilly," the girl said with a shy smile.

"And I'm Anna," she replied, walking toward her.

"It takes a while ta adjust ta the work here, but you'll get used ta it by and by," Lilly said, as she fried strips of bacon for her recipe.

"Well, thank you for the encouragement!" Anna smiled. "You will help me, won't you?"

"Ya mean help ya remember Mrs. Betty's speech?" Lilly tried hard not to laugh. Then her eyes took on a saddened look. "Even I can't remember to be good all the times," Lilly said, looking down at her feet.

"No one is good, Lilly; in the Bible, it says that no one is good, not even one."

Lilly looked up, surprised. "You're saying I'm not the only one that don't do everything right the first time and forgets to do things when they be told?"

"Yes," said Anna. "Many people forget to do those things, because no one is perfect."

"There isn't not nobody that's perfect?"

Anna ignored her incorrect grammar and replied in an earnest tone. "There's only one person in the whole wide world who's perfect, and that person died so you might be saved."

Fear shot into Lilly's eyes. "Ya mean Jesus, don't ya?" she whispered.

Anna looked surprised. "Yes, you know of Him?"

Lilly looked around as if afraid of being overheard. "We ain't allowed to talk of such things here, and if ya know what's good for ya, you'll keep quiet 'bout it too!"

Anna looked at Lilly, a confused expression starting across her face. "I cannot keep silent, Lilly! God has done a work in me He can also do in the lives of others, and some people might not know that they can be saved from the coming destruction!" Anna took a deep breath. "They are perishing and they have only one hope left, and what if I am here to show them that hope—I can't do that if I am silent."

66

Lilly glanced at Anna's face, seeing that Anna was stuck in her ways and nothing was going to change her decision. She turned back to her work. "Very well," she replied with a sigh. "But don't plan on bein' on this earth much longer."

What Lilly meant by that statement, Anna didn't know, but there wasn't time to find out; there was still much work to be done before nightfall. "Where do I find Mrs. Betty?"

As if on cue, Betty walked stiffly into the already hot and humid kitchen. "Why you two a standin' tha for? Did winter come up so quick ya froze mid-step?"

Anna turned towards her and smiled. "I am through with my first task. What else can I do?"

"That's impossible!" Betty exclaimed in astonishment. But upon looking at the dishes and inspecting several of them, she regarded Anna in surprise. "Yeah, ya can take the wash water and dump it to da flower beds ou' back. Lilly will show ya where ta dump um'."

Lilly smiled, clearly happy to get out of the kitchen. Anna grabbed a wash tub and Lilly did likewise. They dumped the heavy tubs of water in the flower beds and made their way back to the kitchen.

This might not be such a bad job after all, Anna thought to herself.

She would work hard and have a cheerful heart, and soon, hopefully things would start to run smoothly.

William sat up in bed, holding his head and releasing a deep moan. He rang the bell by his bedside and a servant came quickly, awaiting his command.

"Please bring me some water, Phillip, and get me something for this headache."

"Yes, massa, I shall have it right up to ya." Phillip made his way out the door, but William stopped him. "Phillip?"

Phillip came back and stood by his master's bedside. "Yes, Your Highness?"

"Did she sign it?" It was a question he had tried to rid himself of all evening; a question he was afraid to know the answer to. But he had to know. He had to ask. And so, he awaited the answer with a trembling heart.

"Yes, sah." Phillip said without emotion. Phillip looked down at the ground as he turned around and stiffly walked out the room.

William sighed as his head fell back against his pillows. He closed his eyes, but he only saw visions. Visions upon visions of servants and slaves being beaten by the hand of his father, the king, and there was nothing he could do to stop any of it.

Anna's day consisted of doing many of the tasks Betty had mentioned in her speech that morning. She didn't have time to think of her encounter with Lilly, or why William had tried to stop her from signing the paper. By nightfall, Anna's back had begun to ache and she was more thankful than ever that it was time to retire for the night.

She spread her mat in the corner of the kitchen, pressed her back up against the cold, hard wall and closed her eyes. She tried to replay all that had happened the last day and a half, but it all seemed so jumbled. It was then that she had time to think. *What caused William's outburst as I began to sign the document? Is he really disturbed because of his mother's death, or is there a deeper, underlying reason?*

Anna knew there was only one Person who would give her the answers she was looking for, and she knew the way to approach Him. So, Anna prayed; she prayed for Lilly, that, wherever she might be, she would be convicted of her sins and see her need for a Savior. She prayed for William and for the king. She prayed for her precious siblings, who seemed so far away. And lastly, she prayed for herself, that God would sort out all the confusing things in her jumbled mind and that she would have the strength to journey on.

Have I made a mistake, Lord? She asked herself. *I felt peace about my decision. Why must I feel doubt now?*

She shifted on her mat, trying to not have a complaining attitude. She couldn't remember the last time she had been so uncomfortable. She wrapped her shawl tighter around her shoulders.

Why am I here? Anna asked herself.

Then, her mother's words came back to her. *'Other times He wants us to be a light and a witness to the perishing, and the perishing usually aren't in the most comfortable of situations, but He sends us to them to be witnesses.'*

"Is there someone perishing here, Lord?" she asked, tears welling up in her eyes. "Is that why I'm here? Is there someone here that needs to know their way out of bondage?"

She thought back to Lilly's words from when they were in the kitchen. *'We aren't allowed to talk of such things here, and if you value your life, you'll keep quiet about it too!'*

"Please, Lord, help me not to shrink from my task of sharing the gift You have given us, just because I value my life."

Well, Anna determined as she lay her head upon her arm and closed her eyes, *if the punishment here for sharing God's love is death, then there's no doubt that I'll be the first victim.*

Little did Anna know the bittersweet truth in that statement.

Seven

Anna's eyes flew open. She lay still, barely breathing, as she tried to find out why she woke up. Then she heard it. A low moaning sound coming from somewhere inside the palace. It had an eerie sound that sent chills through her slight frame.

It began to get louder and louder until Anna couldn't bear it any longer. She quietly stood up from her mat and steadied herself against the cold stone wall. She felt her way throughout the kitchen and stretched her hands out in front of her to keep from bumping into things. She found her way slowly through the spacious room, the moaning increasing with every step.

Anna bumped against a table and stifled a scream. She stepped back and took a deep breath, telling herself how silly it was to be so afraid.

Slowly and carefully, she made her way to the door that led to the long palace hall. She stopped fast, her heart caught in her throat; a figure clothed in white stood in the far corner of the kitchen.

Anna gasped and covered her mouth to keep from screaming. The figure looked up, but Anna still could not see its face clearly. The room was then illuminated with a bright light.

Anna shielded her eyes and stepped back.

"Mornin'," said Lilly, her tone flat.

Anna was so relieved that she gave Lilly a hug, much to Lilly's surprise. "I have never been so glad to hear anyone's voice in my entire life!" Anna exclaimed.

Lilly looked at her. "Alright," she nodded, her voice filled with slight confusion.

Anna helped Lilly prepare an early breakfast for the king.

Because of her scare with Lilly, she failed to realize that the moaning had stopped.

From where or whom the moaning came, she had yet to discover.

King Raymond stood before his window, the darkness of the morning enclosing him as if he were in a cage, trapped against his will. He was hopeless beyond words. He felt as if he were drowning in an ocean and he was the only person in the world. His chin trembled slightly as he thought of his wife. Why had God seen fit to snatch her from his grasp? Why had He taken her away from him? He was surprised at how easily the thoughts concerning God had come to mind. He had tried to banish God from his mind soon after his dear wife's death. He wanted nothing to do with a god who let innocent people die and let harm fall on guiltless victims.

But that was you, his conscience whispered. *You took part in killing a blameless victim.*

"I only made a simple law and it wasn't being followed!" he argued loudly to himself. "She knew the law was punishable by death, but she was too pious to care!"

Breathing heavily, he half-staggered over to his bed. He groaned inwardly as he sat down and buried his face in his hands. Raymond shook his head slowly back and forth, muttering all the while. She had gotten what she deserved. She didn't follow his rules. And when the rules weren't followed, people often got hurt. But something inside of him cried out in protest. *It wasn't just! She didn't deserve to die!*

Raymond stood, clenching his fists in anger. That's how life was. Cruel and unfair. He was only doing his best to live happily from day to day. He couldn't do that if he was being tormented by his conscience with every passing moment.

"*Every* Christian *in this world deserves to die*," he muttered. *They only pollute the world with their lies and hypocritical personalities.* Raymond had gotten his fill of both.

He grasped a small bell sitting upon a table by his bedside and shook it fiercely. A servant answered immediately. His muscular frame and large shoulders gave him an intimidating presence. His black hair was cropped short and only slightly darker than his beard, which was trimmed short against his jaw. He was dressed from head to toe in full body armor, his hand resting lightly upon the sword that hung from a belt by his side.

"Yes, Your Majesty?" He bowed.

King Raymond stood. "I have an assignment for you, Ahmad. It is to be done correctly or not done at all. If it is not done at all, I shall be very angry, and you know what happens when I become angry, do you not?"

The king lifted Ahmad's chin, forcing him to meet his gaze. Ahmad stiffened, but looked him in the eye with defiant confidence, which only served to exasperate the king further. He released his hold rather forcefully and began pacing his bedroom quickly, rubbing his chin in thought. "That new scullery maid has been here for almost two weeks and it's time she's done her part. Here is my command."

Anna set down the bucket of soapy water and stood up to stretch her aching back. Letting out a small sigh, she pressed her fingers against her temples, praying her headache would go away soon.

Lilly came into the kitchen, her face looking a bit more peaceful than it had this morning. Anna could sense something was still bothering her, but felt that it wouldn't be wise to bring it up.

"It be break time," Lilly stated, as she solemnly hung her apron on a hook.

"And not a moment too soon," Anna quipped cheerfully, as she took off her apron and hung it up to dry. "I guess I will soon learn how to wash the house and not myself. I think I'm almost as wet as the floor!"

But Lilly didn't look amused. She glanced down at the floor as she brought her bucket to stand beside Anna's. Anna took a small plate from the stack of clean dishes and placed a piece of ham and a scoop of cold cereal onto her plate. She then went to a small table in the corner of the kitchen and sat down to eat. She didn't feel like praying. She was not at all pleased about the food, and the fact that it was cold was even more bothersome.

Dear Lord, please help me to be thankful, she prayed silently. Folding her hands and closing her eyes, she prayed that the Lord would give her a heart of thanks and take away her complaining attitude.

When she lifted her head and reached for the cold piece of ham, her gaze rested on Lilly. The girl was trembling and looked horrified.

Anna knew the cause of Lilly's trembling, but there was nothing she could do. She couldn't stop praying and giving praise to God just because she feared man, so Anna told her just that.

Lilly gasped and her eyes grew hard. "You must!" she said, her eyes filling with tears. She spun on her heels and quickly left the kitchen.

Ahmad went about his duties that morning with a heavy heart. He knew that what he was doing was very wrong, but he didn't have a choice. Or did he?

He leaned against the wall and looked out over the palace lawn. It was always so immaculate, so precise, so pretty, yet so empty. *Just like me,* he thought. *And nothing I do shall ever fill that void.*

But he was the second hand of the king, and he was paid good money for it. He was committed to King Raymond and he couldn't leave. He had been excited when he heard that he was to work for the king, five years ago to this day.

However, after witnessing the scene almost three weeks ago, his heart had grown hard against the king of Carpathia.

But he had no choice, he convinced himself. No choice at all.

William glanced at the intricate wooden clock standing in the corner of his spacious room and sighed. He couldn't stay hidden forever.

He had been avoiding his father since he had tried to stop Anna from signing, which was almost two weeks ago.

What had possessed him to try to stop her from signing that paper? Why couldn't he just keep his big mouth shut?

William kicked the foot of his bed in anger. "Ouch!" he grumbled, rubbing his foot in pain. But his next thought erased all the pain from his mind. *Because,* his conscience whispered, *you know the anger of your father, and the danger of being under his control.*

William glanced at a painting hanging on his wall, a beautiful lady dressed in a silken blue evening gown with cream-colored satin ribbons. Her hair was taken up in a loose braided bun, leaving only a few golden curls framing her pretty face. A gold crown sat on her head, twisting and turning in the most striking pattern, set with emeralds, sapphires, diamonds, rubies and pearls.

William walked over and fingered the red curtain that hung around the painting. "Even if you were adorned with every precious jewel in the entirety of Carpathia, they would all pale in comparison with your beauty, mother," William said softly.

Queen Isabelle was indeed striking in appearance, but all who truly knew her recognized that her beauty went far beyond her fair skin and delicate complexion. She had as much kindness as a body could possibly hold, and her words of encouragement went far beyond just her family, it also extended to every servant and to everyone she met.

She was loved by all and was never known to have an enemy.

And, when she was still living, her husband always listened to her suggestions, giving her all that her heart desired. If he were in the wrong, she would only look at him with a quiet smile and meekly offer her suggestion. He would listen; he always did. So what changed him?

Maybe it was you, the tempter whispered. *Maybe you are the problem... maybe if you had never been born, the world would be a much better place.*

William glanced around the room—he had half expected someone to be standing there; the voice had seemed so real.

His face paled. What if it *was* his fault? What if the world *would* be better off without him? Maybe he *was* the problem....

William left his room with a heavy heart, the tempter's words never going far from him: *the world would be a better place... if you weren't in it....*

Ahmad crept silently into the kitchen. He crouched behind a low wall so that he couldn't be seen. It was then that he heard Anna's earnest tone. "I can't stop praying, Lilly!"

He heard Lilly gasp, "You must!"

He crouched lower as Lilly sped past him. He watched until he was sure she was out of sight. He wondered if she had noticed him, though it wouldn't do much harm if she had. He suddenly heard Anna speaking again, and he listened quietly. "Dear Lord," she prayed. "Please give me guidance on how to explain my faith to Lilly. She is afraid, Lord, of what, I am not certain. But please calm her anxiety and help her to seek You. She needs You so much. Help me to trust You, Lord, through everything. In Your precious name I pray, Amen."

Ahmad's heart was beating fast in his chest as he deftly stood up and disappeared into the shadows.

Ahmad, trembling, knocked on the door of the king's chamber. The king quickly answered and ushered him in.

"Well?" the king asked impatiently.

Ahmad hesitated a moment before answering, much to the king's displeasure. "She seems to idolize her God," he began slowly.

The king's eyes lit up and he leaned forward so as not to miss a single word. "Yes?" he snapped, "What else?"

Ahmad took a deep breath. "She prays quite often to Him, or so it seems." He paused.

"Well? Is that all?" Raymond yelled, a little louder than he had intended.

Ahmad's eyes took on a wild look and he answered the king quickly. "She knows praying to her God is not allowed. I heard Lilly, the young kitchen maid, tell her so."

The king looked up and rubbed his hands in thought. "And she refuses to stop?" he asked.

"Yes, Your Majesty."

"Now *that* is more interesting!" The king grinned. He had much to think about and didn't need Ahmad any longer.

So, with a flick of his wrist, the king sent him out the room.

"Have you heard of the new scullery maid hired for the king?" asked a middle-aged lady named Sarah to the storekeeper's wife.

Sarah had come into the dry goods store only to relay the juicy gossip she had just overheard.

"No, I haven't," Mandy replied, her eyes growing wide with delight. Walking briskly over to the front door of the mercantile, she flipped over the *open* sign so that it now stated *closed.*
She went back to her friend still standing by the counter and took her gently by the arm. "Come into the parlor. You must tell me all about her!"

Once the two ladies were seated, Sarah began rapidly, "Oh, Mandy, you will never believe what I am about to tell you!" she began. "It's so sad how the poor girl could be taken into the king's wicked trap so easily!"

Mandy poured two cups of steaming hot tea and set out a plate of scones. "Sarah, you must slow down!" she begged. "And start from the beginning."

"Oh, my apologies!" Sarah replied, taking a sip of tea. "So this young girl, she's twenty, perhaps—"

"That's not so young," Mandy interrupted, her tone matter-of-fact.

"Well, maybe she was younger than that!" Sarah snapped. "I don't know her exact age!" She took a deep breath. "As I was saying," she began again, giving Mandy a stern look. "Her name is Anna and she came here to live with her aunt. And you won't ever believe who her aunt is!"

Mandy looked annoyed. "If I will never believe it, then why bother in telling me?"

Sarah sighed, exasperated. "Oh, Mandy, that's just a figure of speech! Do you want to hear the rest of the story or not?"

"Oh, alright, I'll keep quiet!" Mandy sighed, her face taking on a slight pout.

"Good, as I was saying, her aunt is—or I should say *was*, God rest her soul... Jane Willowbee."

"Jane Willowbee!" Mandy gasped. "The poor soul. How did she react to the news of her aunt's death?"

"They say she held up quite well, but I don't think she really knows the truth. She must be so gullible and naïve to take a position working for that monster!"

"Oh, Sarah, how could you make such accusations? You haven't even met her yet!" Mandy spoke reprovingly.

"Well, I'm entitled to my opinions," argued Sarah. "They also say that she's a believer." Her eyes were wide.

Mandy sighed. "Well, she will see where that gets her soon enough."

"She's been there for almost two weeks now," Sarah murmured, more to herself than to Mandy.

"Well, I must get going." She stood up, preparing to leave.

"Thanks for filling me in, Sarah," Mandy replied happily. "You must let me know if you find out anything else!"

"I will. Bye-bye now! I'll see myself to the door."

Mandy heard the familiar jingle of the door as her friend departed, and without meaning to, her thoughts began to wander. She sighed as she thought of the days before Jane's death, as well as the days following it.

Jane was such a sweet soul, always willing to lend a hand or offer a word of cheer. Mandy's thoughts were interrupted by a quick rap on the door. She had forgotten to flip the sign back over! She quickly left her seat to see who it was.

"Oh, Priscilla! How nice to see you! How can I help you today?" Mandy asked, opening the door and flipping the sign over.

"I just need a pound of sugar," replied the energetic girl.

"Alright," Mandy replied. "I'll get it straightaway."

"Oh!" cried Priscilla. "I almost forgot mother's birthday present! What would you suggest?" Her amber-colored eyes curiously looked around the store as she awaited Mandy's response.

"Well, seeing that your mother is a plain, sensible and practical woman... I am sure she would like, um, let's see... anything that's plain, sensible, or practical!" Mandy finished with a flourish.

"Oh," Priscilla said, a bit disappointed. "I'll take a pound of your finest chocolates, and a half-pound of those," she pointed to a bright, colorful display of candy drops.

"Oh, I am sure she will be delighted with your choice!" Mandy exclaimed, happy at the big order. *That is, if she has a sweet tooth like her daughter.* She began wrapping the purchases up for Priscilla, but stopped midway. "Oh, I almost forgot!" Mandy leaned forward, continuing in a whisper. "Have you heard about the king's new scullery maid?"

A loud clanging pot woke Anna with a start.

"Ya only got twenty minutes for ya break and ya've by far exceeded that!" Betty snapped. "What da ya mean by this?" she fumed, stomping her foot to accentuate her words.

"I... I must have fallen asleep, ma'am," Anna stammered. She glanced around, discovering that she must have fallen asleep in the middle of her prayer.

"Yeah," Betty replied in a mocking tone. "Ya *must* have. Ya will take this bucket of soapy water and scrub every fireplace in this palace!"

Getting out of the hot stuffy kitchen was just the thing Anna had hoped for, and she couldn't have had a better punishment, but she still felt a little bad for having fallen asleep.

"I'm sorry, ma'am. I truly am. It won't happen again," she apologized meekly.

"See to it that it don't!" Betty sputtered. She spun around and walked as quickly as her stout body could carry her to a chair in the corner of the kitchen. She sat down with a heavy sigh and grabbed a knife and began chopping a pile of vegetables.

Anna pushed down the unwelcome feelings she had for Mrs. Betty and made her way to the end of the kitchen. The door leading to the rest of the palace stood only feet away. And not too many days away stood a portion of Anna's life she would never forget.

Eight

"When does Father come home, Maman?" asked young Amira.

"Yes, Maman, when?" mimicked Alayla.

She was nearly two years younger than her sister and always followed her sister's example, repeating almost everything she said.

"Same time he comes home every day, children," replied Layla, the girl's mother, in a hurry. She bent down to retrieve a loaf of bread from the oven.

"I don't believe Allah cares about us at all, Maman!" declared Amira, clearly showing she had been thinking on the matter long before she had voiced her opinion.

"You mustn't say that, child!" Layla cried, dropping the loaf of bread onto the counter. She reached down and took Amira's small face between her calloused hands. "You do not want to make Allah angry."

"No, Maman," Amira whimpered, her deep brown eyes filling with tears.

"She didn't mean it, Maman!" cried Alayla, who hated to see her big sister in trouble.

"Hold your tongue, child!" Layla replied, louder than she had intended.

Alayla's body trembled, but she said nothing more.

"Now," Layla commanded, "you must go to your room and repent to Allah!" She pointed to the bedroom Amira shared with her sister.

"Yes, Maman," Amira murmured.

Amira slowly walked to her room and closed the door softly behind her. But not before she heard her mother say in a loud but trembling voice, "Allah, forgive her! She knew not what she was saying!"

But Amira knew what she was saying, even if she didn't fully understand the consequences. Her eyes fillcd with tears and her chin quivered slightly. "I want to believe in Caleb's God," Amira murmured as she knelt beside her cot. Caleb's God seemed to care deeply for him.

She folded her hands in prayer and her lips began to move silently. *Dear God, I don't know Your exact name. I don't know if You are hearing me right now, but Caleb said You saved him from hell, and he didn't have to try to be good all his life to gain entrance into paradise, although he called it heaven, I think. He just had to trust in You and a few other things and he was saved! He is so happy since he got saved. He is happy even though he doesn't have a maman or papa like I do. He's still happy even when his sister Anna had to go miles and miles away from him. I want some of that true happiness too.*

Please help me to understand a little more of what's going on, because it's rather confusing. That's not Your fault! It's just because I don't understand. Please send me a way of understanding it, and a way to learn more about You.

I'm not sorry about what I said about Allah, and I'm not going to repent about it either. Please help Maman not to ask if I did, because I don't want to lie.

Well, I must go now; Mother needs my help.

I hope I didn't take up too much of Your time. Amen.

Amira stood and made her way to the door. She felt strongly at peace about her decision. "I don't believe in you, Allah," Amira whispered. "And I don't believe you have any special powers. I don't even believe you exist!" Amira smiled. "We'll see what becomes of *that!*"

Anna stepped back into the room she had just cleaned. She looked back one last time at the fireplace to see if it was clean enough for Mrs. Betty.

"Well," Anna said, as she picked up her bucket, "it's the best I can do."

She made her way through the many rooms of the palace, stopping occasionally to admire the beautiful artwork. Standing at the top of the giant spiral staircase, her stomach churned as she realized how far up she had gotten. She was not accustomed to such heights; it would take her a while to get used to this.

After another hour of cleaning, she had finally finished.

She made her way to the giant staircase and laughed out loud as she realized that making her way down along with the bucket of water would be as hard as the task she had just accomplished. Coming up was not so hard, but going down was a different story! But Anna always loved a challenge, so she made her way down the stairs with a determined mind.

She soon finished the last fireplace, which happened to be in the library.

Plunging her hands into the dirty, soapy water bucket, she washed them as best as she could and dried them thoroughly on her apron.

She walked noiselessly across the library, her eyes roaming over the many books just beckoning to be read. There were so many that she didn't know where to start. After looking around for a few minutes, she came upon an old, rugged tome, but she couldn't quite make out the words on the spine. The mystery of the 'unreadable' title beckoned to be investigated. She grabbed hold of the book and gave it a tug. But it wouldn't budge.

Anna tugged as hard as she could, but made sure not to damage the book in any way.

As the book gave way, she jumped back with a startled gasp.

Part of the bookshelf started to slide away, a low rumble and creaking sound erupting as the shelf slid open.

She stood still, not daring to move.

Anna dropped onto her knees, trying to get a better look. The smell of musty leather hit her almost as fast as the realization that she was witnessing something much more elaborate than her mind could grasp.

"Books," she whispered in awe. "Not just any books, but *religious* books." Seconds later, Anna exclaimed, "The Bible!" She trembled in delight. It was the first copy she had seen since coming here.

Upon deeper inspection, she realized that there was not only one copy of the beloved Book, but three. Besides that, there were several more leather-backed books, some of which she remembered seeing in her pastor's library back home, others of which she had never seen before.

Her hands shook with excitement as she reached out to retrieve one of the Bibles.

She took a deep breath and gently lifted its cover.

Glancing at the inscription, she noticed it had faded over time and was almost unreadable. She squinted as she tried to make out the words.

To our dearest daughter Isabelle,
Just as you have watched your father work day
unto day with his occupation as master of the
lighthouse, so may your light shine to all the
world!
We love you, daughter!
Love,
Father and Mother

Anna felt as if she had just intruded into a special part of someone's life. She carefully placed the book back onto the shelf.

She picked up another book. "A book of John Bunyan's sermons!" Anna said, fascinated. Caleb would be delighted when he heard of the mystery she had uncovered. She should write them all very soon. No doubt her siblings were wondering of her whereabouts.

She was brought quickly out of her thoughts when she heard footsteps in the hallway.

Her mind began to spin as she realized how dangerous this could be if she were caught. She wasn't doing anything wrong, she argued within herself. And she *had* been given access to the library. But she hadn't been given access to this certain part, she was sure. It was being hidden from someone or something. If the wrong person found out it was here....

Anna's hands trembled as the footsteps grew louder. She reached for the old worn book that had started it all, and gave it a tug, but to no avail. Anna's heart began to race and her hands began to shake. The footsteps stopped, and for a split second, Anna dared to hope that they wouldn't enter the library, but that was a dim hope. Anna's heart sank as she watched the doorknob begin to twist. Her body froze, but her mind was racing.

Oh, dear Lord! she prayed inwardly. *Help me!* She listened closely as a voice could be heard outside the library door.

"Oh, now I remember. I must have left it in my room. Me and my old mind don't get along much anymore."

Anna almost cried as she heard the footsteps retreat.

"Thank you, Lord!" she rejoiced.

She turned back to the hidden shelf, and gasped. She had been so absorbed in the steps of the intruder she didn't notice the hidden shelf had slid back into place.

"Come on, Amira!" Caleb yelled, somewhat impatiently. "We're going to be late!"

Amira's straight black hair blew into her face as she slowed to a stop. "I don't know if this is a good idea, Caleb," she said slowly, taking a deep breath and tucking a strand of wayward hair behind her ear.

"You said you wanted to find out more about God," argued Caleb, "so that's what we are going to do." He came to stand beside her. "I know this isn't an easy decision. But you must keep going. You can't turn back now!"

Amira's voice quivered with emotion. "But what if Father and Mother find out?" she asked, her eyes filling with tears. "I would be in so much trouble!"

She sat down on a rock and folded her hands tightly in her lap.

Caleb sat down beside her and spoke in an earnest, soothing tone. "That's part of the risk we take upon ourselves for putting our trust in the Lord. But it helps to know that whatever may happen, when we die, we shall be with Him forever!"

Strangely, Caleb's words brought a peace to Amira's heart. "So, this is the right decision?" she asked, although it sounded more like a statement.

"Yes," answered Caleb, pulling her to her feet. "Now," he smiled brightly, "we have some answers to get!"

Amira smiled back at him, and they continued on their way to the little white church upon the hill.

William had been ignoring Anna and he couldn't hide it any longer.

I don't usually run into the servants on purpose, he argued within himself.

He knew why he had been avoiding her, and it was even harder admitting it to himself. He couldn't bear to see the state she was bound to be in. No doubt she was pale and terror-stricken. And most of all, she surely hated him for the situation he had gotten her into.

When he ran into her on his way to the library, he was as surprised as the sun would be if it changed into the moon. In fact, he walked right past her and only stopped several paces later, when he spun around and spoke her name as if she were the last person he had ever expected to see.

Anna stepped out of the library with her mind in a whirl.

She walked down the hallway with the water bucket in tow, but she didn't stop to admire the paintings this time. She didn't notice the paintings at all. Her mind was wandering much faster than she could keep up with. *It's so strange,* she mused. *Why would someone lock up all those books? Who would lock them up? And does someone besides me know the books are hidden there?*

Someone would have to, she thought.

These questions, and many more, spun through Anna's mind. She was so absorbed in her thoughts that she failed to notice William as he walked right past her.

She stopped suddenly when she heard her name.

I'm caught! Someone saw me in the library, were Anna's first thoughts.

Getting a hold of herself, she turned around slowly, holding her breath and bracing herself for what was to come.

William quickly closed the gap between them and awkwardly shifted from one foot to another. His mind blanked as he tried to think of something to say, but Anna fixed that for him.

"You didn't tell me you were the prince," she stated, her tone slightly reproving.

William shrugged his shoulders. "I apologize for that, but if you knew how differently people treated you just because of a title, I'm sure you would have done the same thing. That's also why I wasn't dressed in my normal uniform." He took a deep breath. "I completely deserve your hatred, and whatever you must say, you might as well say it now and get it over with."

Anna stared at him in shock. "I hold no hatred toward you at all. Actually, I am very thankful you offered me this position. I'm sure, in time, I shall get used to the change, as it is not exactly what I have been accustomed to."

It was William's turn to be shocked. That wasn't at all what he had been expecting. "I was sure you would have found this place quite depressing," he said, with a sweeping gesture towards the rest of the palace.

"Actually," replied Anna, with a smile, "I have found that much joy and pleasure can be found in the gloomiest of places if we do what it takes to make it so."

William was astonished at her comment. "You're saying," he spoke, his brow furrowed in thought, "that the building is not what makes a place depressing, but rather, the people in it?"

Anna smiled brighter. "Precisely, though darkness *can* make a room seem awfully depressing. In the Bible, it says light chases the darkness away, and it is not only speaking of visual light, but also the light of Christ that shines through us."

William's face fell at her last words. Anger and fright shot into his eyes as he spoke in rapid tones, his voice lowering considerably. "You mustn't speak of such things here!"

"Why does everyone keep saying that?" she snapped. "What is wrong about sharing my faith here? Why must I keep quiet?" Anna's face flushed as she awaited William's answer.

"Because your life depends upon it!" he retorted. He spun on his heel and briskly walked away.

Anna stood still and took a deep breath, trying to calm her trembling body. She hadn't reacted to that in the right way at all.

Why did her life depend upon it?

She picked up her bucket and started back toward the kitchen. Why was everyone so angry and closed off about Christ?

These thoughts were never far from her mind as she worked alongside Lilly and Betty for the rest of the day. That evening, her mind was still spinning as she finished preparing for bed. She sat down on her mat and flipped through the pages of her Bible, taking a quiet joy in the rustling sound they made.

Turning up the lamp, she found the desired page and began to read the words of Paul:

"For I am now ready to be offered, and the time of my departure is at hand.
I have fought a good fight, I have finished my course, I have kept the faith: Henceforth there is laid up for me a crown of righteousness, which the Lord, the righteous judge, shall give me at that day:

*and not to me only, but unto all them also that
love his appearing."*

Flipping to another passage she began to read
again:

*"And fear not them which kill the body, but are
not able to kill the soul: but rather fear Him which
is able to destroy both soul and body in hell."*

*"Jesus said unto her, I am the resurrection, and the
life: he that believeth in me, though he were dead,
yet shall he live...."*

Anna started to place the Bible back into the leather
bag, but in the midst of doing so, a piece of paper
slid out from among its pages.

"I don't remember seeing this before,"
murmured Anna in surprise. She lifted the paper and
tilted it to the light. It was a poem!

As her eyes roamed over the page, a distant
memory came back. One of her and her father. He
had called her from his study, and gently placed this
poem in her hands.

She'd been a lot younger then, and the words
didn't have half the impact as they did now.

*"To give up your life for Christ,
Is something few would chose to do,*

To share the blessed story
Even when it becomes dangerous to pursue,
They care not of themselves,
But others and their souls lost to their god,
Not even when thinking twice that it could end
with their body beneath the sod,
For to die for Christ would be such an honor,
And they're excited to share His story,
Even if it means death on their behalf,
To them they deem it glory,
There are but few who would give their life
For sharing a story about Gods love,
But as they're martyred for their faith,
They'll soon be smiling up above."

A.C.I

Anna was quiet for a time, her thoughts lost in the words of the poem.

As Anna lay down to sleep, her mind wouldn't be still.

Where was the mysterious moaning coming from? And why did someone find it necessary to keep the books about God hidden?

Nine

Anna awoke in the middle of the night with the sudden realization that something wasn't right.

Laying as still as she could, she took a deep breath and tried to find the reason for her awakening. Then she heard it: the low moaning coming from somewhere deep within the palace.

Anna stood up; she wouldn't let it slip through her grasp, not this time. She would solve this mystery once and for all.

She found it was much easier to find her way through the kitchen in the dark, having done it before.

The closer she got to the end of the kitchen, the louder the moaning became. She stepped out of the kitchen and closed the door softly behind her. She stood still, trying to decide which way to go. The moaning hadn't stopped and it sounded as if it were coming from somewhere at the top of the palace.

Please guide my steps, Lord, and show me the right way to go.

She walked toward the spiral staircase and began the long trek up. She walked slowly and quietly, but with determined steps. Halfway up, a stair let out a loud creak and Anna froze. She held her breath, hoping no one had heard. She grasped the railing tightly and walked briskly up the rest of the stairs.

The moaning was definitely louder, and Anna let out a sigh of relief knowing that she was on the right track, but it lasted only for a moment. She was making her way toward the mysterious sound when voices erupted through the dimly lit hallway.

Anna gasped quietly as she slipped behind a large potted plant. She held her breath as the voices grew louder.

"I'm out of ideas, Moriah," spoke a hushed voice. "Nothing seems to help."

Moriah asked in hushed tones, "Do you think she has gone mad?"

Anna put her hand over her mouth as they stopped beside her. She backed up closer to the wall, rustling the leaves of the plant. She closed her eyes in dread, her heart beating faster than she thought was possible. *Oh, Lord,* Anna prayed silently, *I need your help more than ever now! Please shield me!* Anna felt sick when she heard the voices again.

106

"Shhh! did you hear that, Silvia?" Moriah asked.

"No, what did it sound like?"

"Like a rustling of some sort."

"This palace makes all sorts of eerie sounds. I'm sure it was just a draft."

Anna sighed in relief as she heard them walk away. For how long she stood there, she didn't know.

When she finally summed up the courage, she quietly slipped out from behind the plant.

She was getting closer now. She could almost feel it.

She stopped when she saw a soft light coming from a room at the end of the hall. She slowly crept forward until she was only a foot away from the door.

The moaning was definitely coming from inside. She cracked the door and peered into the room.

A gasp escaped Anna's lips as she quickly stepped inside.

Anna stood still within the room, waiting for her eyes to adjust to its brightness.

There, in the corner of the room, sat an elderly lady reclined upon a chair, her hands grasping her head tightly. She was writhing and sobbing, making for a pitiful sight.

Anna made sure she was the only occupant in the room before making her way to the lady. When she was within two feet from her, Anna reached out and placed a hand upon her arm. The lady looked up at her, with eyes full of fear. She spoke in rapid sentences, "You've come to take me away! You can't! You can't! I'm not ready to go! I'm not a good person! I'm not ready. I'm not ready!"

Anna was afraid someone would overhear the lady, so she crouched down beside her, talking in a soothing tone. "No one is going to take you away." Anna hoped that was true. "You are safe here. The Lord will watch over you. You are safe within His care." Anna took a deep breath and quietly began to sing.

"There is a land of pure delight,
Where saints' immortal reign;
Infinite day excludes the night,
And pleasures banish pain.

There everlasting spring abides,
And never-with'ring flow'rs;
Death, like a narrow sea, divides
This heav'nly land from ours.

The lady looked up into Anna's hazel eyes. "So, it's true?" she asked, tears glistening in her eyes. "I won't be in this awful world forever? There is a place that has flowers that never fade? How do I get there?"

Anna started in surprise at the lady's sudden change. "If you place your faith in the Lord Jesus Christ, repent of your sins and believe He is the one true way to salvation, then yes, you shall see Him someday in heaven."

The lady whispered, "You won't kill me if I speak of these things?"

Anna stood up and backed away. "Kill you?" Her tone was filled with incredulity. "Why would I kill you?"

The lady stared up at Anna, confused. "They said I would be killed if I keep mentioning the Lord." Her eyes filled once again with terror.

"You know of Him?" Anna asked her. "The one true God?"

The lady nodded sadly. "A little," she whispered hoarsely. "But I don't know how I must be saved, and I am terribly afraid I shall die before I get a chance to learn more about Him! I keep asking them, but they won't answer my questions. They said I shall be killed if I ask again!"

Anna sat down again by the lady. "*Who* has threatened to kill you, and who are *they*?"

Surprise cut across the lady's face; the look she gave Anna said she should have already known. "The king and his servants!" she replied, answering both questions at once.

"Well," replied Anna, with a smile, "we seem to be alone right now—would you like me to tell you about Him, and what you must do to be saved?"

The lady let out an exclamation of delight and sat forward in rapt attention. At last, she had found someone to explain the answers to her questions, and Anna had found a pair of listening ears which longed to hear the story of redemption.

"I'm Agnes," announced the lady, reaching out a withered hand to grasp Anna's.

"And I'm Anna," she replied, smiling. "Is there anything specific you would like to know?" she asked kindly.

"Oh, everything!" Agnes exclaimed.

"Well," Anna began, "many years ago, the world was black and dark. But from the words of the one and true God, the darkness turned to light...."

Anna went on to tell Agnes all about the story of creation, the flood, and most importantly, the sacrifice and resurrection of the one true Lord. Agnes listened, leaning forward so that she would not miss a single word. Her eyes filled with tears as she learned what the Savior did for her, and it was Anna's turn for tears when Agnes gave her life to Christ.

Anna promised to come again soon. She gave Agnes a hug and turned to leave, but Agnes placed a gentle hand on her arm and looked up into Anna's face. In her wobbly voice, now full of happiness and joy, she spoke simple words that Anna would never forget.

"Now there are two lights in this old palace, aren't there?"

Tears glistened in Anna's eyes as she responded. "Yes, Mrs. Agnes, there are, and we must pray that many, many more may come, so that all darkness shall be chased away."

William awoke to the sound of soft footsteps, and his brow wrinkled in confusion as he slipped out of bed. His blanket fell to the ground as he grabbed a red robe trimmed with gold and slipped it over his shoulders. He cracked open his door just wide enough to see through it. His breath caught as he saw Anna's unmistakable figure disappear around the corner. He wondered if he should follow her, but decided against it and sat back down on his bed, a bit unsettled.

Why would she be up at this hour? William asked himself. The clock had struck two a little over a half hour ago. Then he sat straight up, realization hitting him fast.

"Grandmother! She's quiet!" William leapt from his bed and quickly ran up the stairs toward his grandmother's room. Dread spread through William, and he found it difficult to breathe. He felt as if something had just happened, something he could not explain.

His legs felt like lead as he found his way to his grandmother's room. He had been there many times, but it all looked so strange in the dark. A soft light shone from the room as William cracked open her door. He stepped back in surprise as he heard his grandmother's unmistakable voice, but something was different; no longer was it filled with the terror he had heard every night, but peacefulness. His eyes filled with fear as he heard her words.

"And, dear Lord, thank You for saving me tonight! Thank You for sending me answers that helped guide me to the truth. Thank You for taking

the punishment I deserve. Thank You for my dear friend Anna. May You bless her just as she has blessed me. And please help my grandson, William, find the hope I now have. In Your Holy name, Amen." Agnes climbed into her bed and let out a content sigh. "Oh, and thank You, Lord, for finally giving me peace." She closed her eyes, and, with a peaceful smile on her lips, she drifted off to sleep.

William clenched his hands as he briskly walked back to his room.

"How dare she come and cast a spell upon this house with her witchery!" he muttered in anger.

But deep down, he knew his anger was not directed at Anna. He was frightened and scared of what this would mean, of what danger this would bring, not only on Anna, but also his dear grandmother. And he was confused at the change that had come upon his grandmother. She said someone had taken her place.

Was that the same person who took mine? It couldn't be, William tried to reason as he lay back down upon his bed, *because he died for me years ago.*

His mind replayed his last talk with his mother.

"I want that peace," William spoke into the quiet of the room. "I want what mother had, and what grandmother has just discovered. But how?" A tear made its way down William's cheek. He thought of the wicked things he had done in his past and fear crept into his heart.

"Maybe I'm too wicked," he whispered. "Maybe it's too late...."

Another week passed quickly for Anna; another week of hard work and slight confusion. Although she had been very busy, the hidden shelf still consumed much of her attention. She began to understand why they were hidden, but by whom, she had yet to discover.

This was her third week at the palace and she thought it was time she wrote a letter home. She fingered the precious slip of paper containing the address where her brothers were staying. Once Caleb received the letter, he would gather his sisters together and they would have a joyous time, Anna was sure. She smiled as she imagined their reaction.

When evening finally came, Anna sat down upon her mat and withdrew her writing supplies.

She chewed on the side of her lip in thought and finally set her pencil upon the paper:

My dearest brothers and sisters,

How long the days have seemed without your loving companionship, and drearily have the hours gone by....

Anna paused, looking at the words written on the paper. She was not very pleased at what she had written and had a mind to start over.

"It doesn't seem quite appropriate to write something so gloomy," she muttered, folding the piece of paper and putting it back into her box. She felt bad about wasting it, but it wouldn't be wasted, she told herself. She would use it for something soon. She grabbed a fresh sheet and began to write again.

Dear Caleb, Margret, Juliana and Isaiah,

How I have missed you all and each of your sweet personalities! I hope you have not missed me too dreadfully. I pray for each of you every day and hope you have not been too much trouble for the kind families who have opened their homes to you.

I can hardly grasp the fact that we have been parted for almost two months now! You will find it hard to believe what the Lord has been seeing me through lately....

Ten

Anna woke earlier than usual the next morning. She wanted to give her precious letter to Thomas, the servant who delivered the mail and attended to other duties in town.

Anna reasoned that if she mailed the letter today, it should arrive in France in about three to four weeks. That was how long it took her aunt's letter to arrive.

She pulled her hair back with a strip of white cloth. The cloth was not the most elegant in appearance, but it served its purpose in keeping Anna's hair out of her face.

Using the reflection from a nearby pot, she began tucking a few straying strands of hair into the head wrap, but stopped, her hands frozen in mid-air and her brow furrowing in slight alarm.

Her stomach felt sick as she stared at the reflection of her features, features that, she'd been told, slightly mirrored those of her aunt's. Poor Aunt Jane. Anna hoped she hadn't died alone.

It hit her for the tenth time since her arrival, that she didn't even know how her aunt had died. She was old, and she had always been in good health. But she hadn't known who to ask.

Grabbing her valise, she withdrew the letter.

She would try to find out more soon, but she'd have to find someone to ask first.

She reached far within her valise and pulled out a small leather bag. Untying the two strings, she withdrew her last coin. It should be enough to mail the letter, with maybe some left over.

She dreaded the walk to the slave's quarters outside the palace, knowing it would be dark and cold, but there was no other way to get the letter to Thomas. So, with determined steps, she walked through the kitchen, grabbed a lantern and lit it before she left. She closed the door behind her and made her way across the palace lawn.

She could barely make out the silhouette of the buildings serving as houses for the rest of the servants. Anna was half glad she was required to sleep in the kitchen. At least she didn't have to make the trek all the way up to the kitchen every morning.

"Where did Lilly tell me Thomas stayed?" Anna asked herself as she held the lantern high in front of her. She decided to go and ask Lilly herself. She hoped the young girl might be awake and wouldn't be too grumpy by her early morning visit.

Anna stepped up to the second cabin she passed and started to knock on the door. But she heard a soft crying inside that went straight to her heart. Slowly opening the door, her eyes quickly took in the scene before her.

She noticed right away that the cabin consisted of one room. The room was not large, but it was neat and tidy. There was a built-in fireplace, and a small table that sat in one corner with a few wicker chairs placed around it. A shelf above the stove finished the room off nicely.

But what Anna noticed more than anything else was a mat in the corner of the room. Her heart filled with pity as she listened to the scene unfold before her...

Lilly sat on her knees before a woman in her mid-forties. The woman was laying on the mat and moaning pitifully. They had not noticed Anna, so she stayed where she was, her body halfway through the door, her hand resting lightly upon the frame.

"But, Momma," spoke Lilly, "there ain't nothin' I can do ta ease yer sufferin'?" Tears filled her voice as she clung to her mother's hand.

"No child," her mother answered softly. "There ain't nothin' no human could do fer me. Now, you get yerself on back to bed. Ya need the little rest ya can get."

But Lilly wouldn't move. "Momma! What 'bout thet medicine the doctor done gave you awhile back. Didn't that help ya some?"

"Yes, child, but I've done and used it all up and we don't got no mo' money!" She moaned again and Lilly stared sadly at the form by her side.

Without any warning, Lilly let out an exclamation of delight as she hopped up quickly and ran a few feet away. She grabbed a small box from a shelf and rummaged through it until she found what she was looking for. Running back to her mother, she dropped to her knees. "See!" she cried in delight. "I've been savin' it, Momma, for somethin' special." Lilly's eyes sparkled as she displayed the coin in the middle of her dark palm.

Josie's eyes softened as she understood the sacrifice it was for her daughter. But it wasn't enough.

"It ain't enough, Lilly child," her mother said gently as she shifted so she could see her daughter's face.

Lilly's heart sank, her voice losing much of its eagerness. "How much we be lackin', Momma?" she asked softly.

Lilly's face fell as her mother answered.

Anna softly closed the door on the saddening scene and unclasped the hand tightly holding her last coin. Anna knew at once what she must do.

"She needs it more than I," she whispered softly as she made her way back to the palace.

She tried not to think about what it would mean if she gave up the last of her money, but as she arrived back at the palace and closed the door upon the morning light, a verse began to creep into Anna's mind and heart:

"But whoso hath this world's good, and seeth his brother have need, and shutteth up his bowels of compassion from him, how dwelleth the love of God in him?"

Anna needed no more urging as the Lord brought this scripture to mind. Placing her precious letter back into the bag once again, she withdrew the piece of scrap parchment. Grabbing her pencil, she wrote something upon the paper, then folded the piece of paper this way and that until it resembled a small pocket.

She thought how proud her little brother would be if he knew how she had finally found a use for one of his folding tricks.

Placing the coin into the parchment pocket, she flipped down the top so it wouldn't slip out. She then retraced her steps outside until she was again at the door of Lilly's cabin. There was no need for the lantern, for the sun had once again began its trek up into the sky.

She softly ascended the few stairs and slid the pocket quietly under the cabin door.

The sun cast its beautiful rays upon the clouds, making them glow with soft pinks and purples. The tall mountains reflected in the silvery lake below, making for a breathless picture indeed. Birds chirped their early morning song, inviting Anna to join them.

Her soul began a song that lifted her spirits high above the mountains as she joined the merry birds in the glorious melody.

Praise to the Lord, the Almighty,
The King of Creation
O my soul, praise Him,
For He is thy health and salvation!
All ye who hear,
Now to His temple draw near,
Join me in glad adoration!

Praise to the Lord,
Who doth prosper thy work
And defend thee;
Surely His goodness and mercy
Here daily attend thee.

Ponder anew what the Almighty can do,
If with His love He befriend thee.

Praise to the Lord,
O let all that is in me adore Him!
All that hath life and breath,
Come now with praises before Him.
Let the Amen sound from His people again,
Gladly for aye we adore Him.

Anna thought of the phrase from the verse she had just sung, *ponder anew what the Almighty can do,* and she chided herself for not pondering the marvelous things the Lord was doing in this dismal palace.

Had He not saved Agnes and taken care of her every need?

So it was that Anna's morning had been granted a generous dose of joyfulness, and her heart and mind were granted peace, a peace that couldn't be explained, no, not even if she were given a thousand words to choose from. But that didn't matter to Anna; she had peace and joy, and for the time being, she was content to rest under the shadow of her Savior's comforting wing.

Lilly sat under the shade of a giant magnolia tree, busily sewing a tear in her little sister's dress.

"I can't count the times I've done mended up Sally's dresses!" she complained. But inwardly she knew if her mother were well, she wouldn't be the one mending any of her little sister's clothes.

At the thought of her mother, Lilly's face fell. She was tired of her mother's sickness and she was also tired of taking up the slack and doing not only her own work but also much of her mother's. Everyone knew if the work wasn't getting done, the slave masters would soon find out why.

Lilly looked forward to the day when they could all be free. Freedom was a word all children knew. It held power and meaning, but Lilly had yet to find out what this very powerful word meant.

"God," Lilly whispered to herself, *"Anna says You're real, and Ya care 'bout us, and when we got trouble to ask Ya. Well, I'm askin' Ya, I'm beggin' Ya, please send some way fer Momma to get well and strong again, please send us help."*

Lilly looked around in fear, lest anyone had overheard her quiet petition. It had taken much courage to do what she had just done, especially after what she had witnessed only a couple weeks ago.

Lilly trembled as she remembered the frightening scene.

A shout in the distance brought Lilly out from her thoughts. She looked up from her sewing as her little sister ran toward her waving a white object up in the air. "Lilly!" Sally cried in delight. "Look what *I* found," she said, placing her prize upon Lilly's lap.

Lilly carefully unfolded the paper as she began questioning her little sister. "Where'd ya find it, Sally?" Lilly asked, looking her little sister in the eye.

"By the door."

But it couldn't have been, thought Lilly. She had come out of the door this morning. Unless it had been placed there *after* she went out—she had gone out quite early to watch the sunrise.

"Got it!" she exclaimed, as the paper pocket slid open, revealing a message. She gasped when a coin fell out into her lap.

Lilly grasped the coin in her hands, not daring to speak. What if her prayer had been answered? She had taken such a risk in even thinking of God, but what if He actually heard her prayer?

Lilly's hands trembled as she picked up the coin. Tears filled her eyes as she figured that combined with her money she had saved, it would be enough to pay for her mother's medication. She was so filled with delight over the coin that she hadn't even given a thought to the message written inside of the paper.

"What's it say?" questioned little Sally, as she gave a gentle but determined tug to the sheet of oddly folded paper.

Lilly pulled it back from her and began to read silently, ignoring Sally's protests to read aloud.

"Give, and it shall be given unto you; good measure, pressed down, and shaken together, and running over, shall men give into your bosom. For with the same measure that ye mete withal it shall be measured to you again." Luke 6:38

Lilly's face froze as she looked at her little sister. "It...it don't say nothin', Sally," she lied. "It doesn't say anything at all...."

She quickly shoved the paper into her dress pocket along with the coin and stood to leave.

"But I saw words!" Sally protested. "Read um' ta me!" she begged, giving Lilly's brown cotton dress an impatient tug.

"Now look, Sally," Lilly said, "if you go and be a good little girl, I'll go and get ya some sweets, how'd ya like that?"

"I like it lots!" she exclaimed joyfully, a smile brightening up her small face.

Lilly ran back to her cabin and quietly went in so as to not wake her mother. She grabbed her coin from the small box upon the shelf and made her way back outside. Walking quickly to the stables, she hoped she wouldn't be too late to catch Thomas before he went to town.

She saw the stables up ahead and soon entered through the giant wooden doors with Sally still at her heels. "Go play, Sally," Lilly yelled impatiently, "or I shan't get you no treats ever!"

Sally's face fell, but she ran off as she was told. Lilly was relieved to see Thomas tacking up Old Glory, one of the black stallions.

"Thomas," she yelled loudly, even though she was quite near him now.

Thomas jumped back, startled, with a surprised expression on his aging face. "What you be wantin', Lilly child?" he asked her kindly.

"I be wantin' you to get more medicine for my momma," she said, holding out her two beloved coins.

Thomas let out an exaggerated whistle and took the shiny coins in his dark calloused palm.

"Where'd you be getting such money, child?" he asked her suspiciously.

"It was given to me," Lilly replied simply. And because he had never known her to tell a lie, Thomas believed her.

"Well," Thomas went on slowly, "I guess I could do dat fer' ya."

Lilly filled him in on what medicine to get and to purchase a little sweet for Sally.

"And don't forget to bring back the extra money," Lilly reminded him as he mounted his horse.

"I's won't ferget, child," he laughed, as he turned his horse around and started off at a brisk trot.

Lilly's heart was filled with happiness as she went back to the palace to start the preparations for the noonday meal.

As she entered the kitchen, she noticed Anna, hard at work, peeling a bowl of potatoes and carrots. Anna hummed happily and looked up, offering Lilly a smile. Lilly smiled back and quickly went to work on a pile of dishes that sat waiting to be washed.

"Where's Mrs. Betty?" Lilly asked Anna after a while.

"She wasn't feeling too well. She said something about her back aching. I finally convinced her to lie down for a short bit."

Lilly didn't reply to Anna's comment. She was too busy thinking of her mother's happy reaction when she would place the medicine into her hands.

She tried to wait patiently, but it was much harder than she could admit.

She worked very diligently for another hour and a half and couldn't help but let out an exclamation of delight when she saw Thomas's familiar form entering through the palace gate. She quickly set down the knife she'd been using to chop apples and ran out into the yard.

Anna smiled to see her go, for she knew what made the child so happy this morning. Lilly hadn't mentioned her discovery, but Anna told herself she would gain Lilly's trust sooner or later.

Lilly's mother was so delighted with the medicine that she hugged Lilly over and over again, exclaiming she was "the best child that ever done lived."

Sally jumped up and down when Lilly presented her with the peppermint sticks and promised to share them with the other children.

Lilly clasped the remaining money in her fist as she carefully planned what to do with it. She also had to find out what to do with the message that was still hiding deep within her dress pocket. She had to find some way to get rid of it. If someone found out that she had been reading even this one small verse of the Bible, she would be in big trouble.

"I wish I never learned to read," she muttered. But she knew it was a privilege to have been taught how to read. When her former slave master's daughter took a fancy to her, she had taught Lilly not only how to read, but also how to do simple math as well. Whatever Carrie had learned in school that day she came home and shared with Lilly.

"I wish I didn't know what a Bible was, then!" she muttered angrily. The Bible had been a forbidden book since she was three. She remembered little about it, but all that needed to be known was that it was a forbidden book. Regardless of its past, it was not to be read, nor spoken of.

Lilly wondered why, but never had the courage to ask. She went back to the palace, wondering what jobs Mrs. Betty had lined up for her next.

"I know what I'll do!" Lilly laughed happily. "I'll give the rest of the money to Mrs. Betty to get herself somethin' nice."

Happy with her idea, she stopped at Mrs. Betty's cabin before returning to the palace.

Stepping up to the door, she folded the paper just as she had found it and slid the coins into the pocket it made. Then she quietly slid it under the door and ran back to the palace. There was no way she would be caught handing forbidden messages around.

Well, she definitely wasn't the one who started it. Anyway, it was Mrs. Betty's problem now.

She really didn't have to guess who started it all. Who else but Anna would take such a risk in passing scriptures around?

But why would she *want* or even *care* about helping her?

These questions burned through Lilly's mind until she could bear it no longer. She had to know, she had to ask, but she had to wait until just the right moment.

And, for Lilly, that was going to take a while.

Betty sat up as she heard a soft sliding noise at her cabin door.

Walking over to the door, she was in the midst of opening it when she noticed an object lying on the floor. She stooped to pick it up. It took much effort, but finally she had the object in her hands.

She shuffled over to an old chair in the corner of the room, and by the light of a candle, she began to examine the object. It took her a fair amount of time, but she finally succeeded in opening it, and to her surprise, out slid a few coins onto her starched apron.

But what surprised her even more was the note inside.

Betty stared wide-eyed at the scripture, reality sinking in.

"Give, and it shall be given unto you; good measure, pressed down, and shaken together, and running over, shall men give into your bosom. For

with the same measure that ye mete withal it shall be measured to you again." Luke 6:38

So, thought Betty, *if I give these coins to someone I will get even more coins back!* She was not normally a very greedy person, but in her haste, she misjudged the Scripture, and so, she began to carry out her plans.

She would give these to someone, she decided. And she knew just the person to give them to.

She hurried back to the palace kitchen with renewed strength.

She was quite delighted when she noticed no one was there.

Walking quickly over to where Anna kept her mat and her few possessions, she slipped the coins into Anna's valise.

But curious Betty couldn't leave it at that, for the bag of Anna's belongings was just too tempting. She opened the valise wider and stared in disbelief as she withdrew a black leather-bound copy of the Bible. Betty gasped as she heard Anna's and Lilly's voices coming toward the kitchen.

She stuck the Bible back into Anna's bag as fast as she could. Then, as quickly as her stout legs could carry her, she walked over to the other side of the kitchen and thrust her big arms into a pot of soapy water.

Anna and Lilly both entered the kitchen laughing over something, but quickly stopped when they saw Mrs. Betty. Betty didn't seem to notice as she plunged a dish into the clean water and set it off to the side to dry.

Anna and Lilly both exchanged curious looks, but left it at that. They worked in silence until the bell rang to serve the royal family their dinner, which meant a fifteen-minute break for Anna.

She decided to spend her time outside.

Her break flew by too quickly, and before Anna knew it, she was once again back at work inside the confines of the palace.

Anna leaned her weary back against the wall and closed her eyes.

It was another end to another day and Anna's body was aching for rest.

She grabbed the valise to get out her Bible, when she heard a clinking noise inside.

Her interest aroused, she took out the contents of her bag. To her surprise, she found three shiny coins resting happily in the bottom.

She stared in disbelief as she counted out the money. Tears filled her eyes as she knew this had been no mistake—there was exactly enough money to send her letter!

How could this have been? Anna asked herself over and over again.

She didn't know. But what she *did* know was that whatever the circumstances...

"Nothing is impossible with God."

Eleven

 A cloud of dust went up into the morning sky. Anna, broom in hand, gave the dusty rug another hard whack. She coughed as the wind blew the dust in her face.

She noticed Lilly steadying her mother as they walked out into the bright afternoon sun. *Lilly has been so happy the last few days,* Anna thought to herself. Since Lilly had bought the medicine, her mother had rapidly regained her strength. Anna waved happily at them when they looked her way.

As Anna sent another plume of dust flying, she thought it was high time she met with Grandmother again. The elderly lady had begged Anna to call her Grandmother, as she had only one grandson and had always wished for a granddaughter. Anna made a mental note to visit her again this evening. She had met with the dear woman a handful of times since their first encounter almost two weeks ago.

They could only meet at night though, and even then, Anna had to be cautious.

Anna thought sadly at the state William was in. He had seemed so kind when she first met him, always willing to help and lend a hand. But he seemed to be concerned and distressed about something. She would occasionally pass him in the palace hall, but she never stopped to speak with him.

She had not dared to breathe a single word about the hidden shelf in the library. And she had not found the right opportunity to ask Grandmother about it yet.

Anna went back into the kitchen, hanging the broom upon its hook in the closet. Anna yearned for a trip to the city. She had no money to spend there, for she only got paid at the end of each month, but anywhere else would be more welcome than the gloomy palace. How she was to get there, or even find the time to get there, Anna had yet to discover.

Mrs. Betty entered the kitchen, and Anna noted with curiosity that she was in quite a happy mood. Anna offered her a bright smile as she passed, and to Anna's great surprise, it was returned.

She shook her head slightly, wondering what had come over Mrs. Betty but she soon gave up trying to find out.

The rest of the day seemed to drag by for Anna. Supper had already been served and the slaves had retired to their quarters for the night. Anna waited until she was sure no one would be stirring before she made her way to Grandmother's room and quietly slipped in. Agnes was reclining in her favorite chair by the window, her face lighting up with great delight as Anna entered. Anna embraced the dear lady and sat down upon a low chair by her feet.

"I'm very happy to have met you, Mrs. Agnes," Anna started, "for I get tired of having only myself to talk to."

"But my dear," Agnes argued, "you don't have only yourself to talk to, you have *God!*"

Grandmother's gentle correction and childlike faith brought Anna back to counting her blessings.

"You're right, I should be thankful I have such an eager listener to speak to any time I want." She then went on to tell Agnes of her day, though it was quite uneventful. She listened closely as Agnes shared with her the little things the Lord had shown her the past few days.

"Did you bring your Bible?" Agnes asked eagerly, her eyes shining as she spoke.

"Oh no!" Anna's voice filled with remorse. "I knew I was forgetting something!" Anna felt truly sorry as she apologized again.

"That's all right, dear," Agnes answered, patting Anna's hand gently. "You can bring it next time."

But Anna couldn't help but notice the sad light that had crept into her dear friend's eyes.

Anna talked to her awhile longer. With a hug and promise to return soon, she left the dear lady in the silence of her room at the top of the palace.

But Anna had a plan, a surprise she was going to share with Agnes. She only had to get it, which was going to take a good bit of thought.

A quick rap on the king's chamber startled him from his frightening dream. He carelessly threw back the coverlet and slipped one of his gold-trimmed robes over his broad shoulders.

With haste, he walked toward his door, but not before laying a cautious hand on the dagger hanging by his side.

He swung open his bedroom door and let out an exclamation of surprise as he looked into the face of his only son.

"Father," William began nervously, as he folded his hands and then dropped them by his side, unsure of what to do with them. "We need to talk."

Astonishment visibly showed on the king's face as he stood still, as if in shock. Talking to his son was the last thing on his list of things to do, but as a thought struck his mind, he opened the door wider and motioned for William to come in.

A sly smile slid across his face. "Indeed we do, my son, indeed we do."

(Thirty minutes earlier)

William paced his bedroom in a perplexed manner, his youthful face showing obvious confusion and distress.

There was something going on within the palace. He could feel it, as if it were a heavy woolen blanket draped across his very soul. He sat down on his bed and stood back up immediately. He continued his pacing, talking to himself all the while. "What's going on?" he asked himself for the fifth time since retiring to his room that evening. A sickening feeling started in the pit of his stomach. He knew it had to do with Anna.

"How could I have been so stupid?" he spoke aloud. He looked at his shiny black boots as he walked in circles around his room. If something happened to Anna, it would be his fault entirely.

"How could I live with that guilt for the rest of my life?" William whispered into the silence of his room.

"Nothing's going to happen," he convinced himself. "Not if I have anything to do with it."

"I will speak to Father!" William determined. But the thought itself made his stomach sick.

He looked down at the ground, his thoughts taking him far away.

Whack!

William let out a groan as he lifted a hand to rub his throbbing head. Another groan escaped his lips, not from pain this time, but more from the fact that he had walked into a stationary object.

"Who put that wall there, anyway?" he muttered, but he knew he was fighting a one-sided argument. Walls don't talk.

He walked toward the door leading out of his room, knowing what he had to do. He dreaded it, but he had to do it.

As he could tell, there was no other way.

"Well?" the king spoke almost kindly, his eyes searching his son's face, seeming to look into the depths of his being.

William was taken aback by his father's curious manner. *He's up to something,* William thought. *But what does he want from me?*

William coughed, trying to gain a few extra seconds. He took a deep breath and began his first tactic. "Well, you see, Father," he started. But then he stopped and began from a different direction. "I was wrong in wanting you to hire that scullery maid."

His father's eyebrows shot up, clearly showing his son's words were not what he had expected.

"She's no good to you," William went on. "I will gladly pay for her voyage back to her homeland, if you so wish it." He held his breath, awaiting anxiously for his father's response.

The king stared at his son and began to grate his teeth, a habit he did when thoroughly upset, and a habit he showed no sign of surrendering.

The sound echoed through the king's chamber, making William shiver slightly. He pushed the sound from his mind and awaited his father's reply.

Time ticked by as the two pairs of eyes locked together. William stood firm and his eyes never wavered from his father's cold stare. But the king wasn't to be challenged, and his anger was slowly bubbling to the surface.

William watched his father take a deep breath, who was also trying to keep his own anger at bay.

"It was *your* doing in hiring that scullery maid," the king said. "Her kind is always getting into mischief."

His face was masked with an almost kindly look, but William had been around his father long enough to know the dark emotions that were just under the surface.

William didn't want a replay of the event so firmly carved into his mind. He didn't want the guilt, the shame and the horrible memories that haunted him, waking him from a fitful sleep.

Courage swept through William's veins. "I won't stand by and watch you do such wickedness again!" William's tone was so firm and demanding that, for a moment, his father was taken aback by his son's audacity. But the king wasn't to be challenged. William's courage rose as he went on. "You've done enough wickedness to last three lifetimes." William's eyes were etched with anger.

For one fleeting moment, the king knew what it felt like to be under someone's submission, to be talked down upon.

And for that one moment, William knew the feeling of being the one to tell and not be told. For one short moment, William felt triumphant.

As he opened his mouth to say more, his father grasped the collar of William's shirt without a single warning. William struggled, but the king's grip only tightened. "You are nothing but a filthy piece of rubbish!" the king spat in William's face. "You have caused nothing but pain to me since the moment you were born!" The king kept a firm grip on William's shirt as he went on. "You brought this scullery maid here on your own accord. I loathe her kind and desire to see them all wither! This is all your own fault," the king sputtered as he forcefully let William go. "And you're going to pay dearly for it!"

William staggered backwards, breathing heavily, his heart beating fast within his chest.

He stepped back slowly, feeling behind him for the door. Finding the handle, he quickly turned it, fleeing from his raging father.

His father's harsh words burned deeply into his heart and mind.

"And you're going to pay dearly for it..."

Twelve

Anna found Thomas right after breakfast. She needed to ask a favor of him and knew just where he'd be.

Having stayed up late working the previous evening, she had gained herself three free hours. She was half-afraid Mrs. Betty would not agree to her plan, but Mrs. Betty didn't seem to care either way, much to Anna's amazement.

Anna entered the stable and saw Thomas. A smile lit his face when he caught sight of her. He was saddling up Old Glory, getting ready to make a trip into town. "Mornin', missy," he said in a lively tone. "What brings ya to see poor Thomas this sunny day?"

Anna gave him one of her well-known smiles and gently leaned on one of the stall railings. "I was wondering if you might be so kind as to let me ride into town with you?" she asked sweetly, her eyes begging for a positive response.

Thomas couldn't resist her smile, nodding his head toward a white stallion standing in the corner of the stable.

Anna thanked him and quickly went to saddle the beautiful stallion. She was soon finished and they headed toward the town.

What Anna was about to do would change her life forever.

William was not weak. He didn't break easily, but his father had pushed him too far this time. And when the prince was pushed too far, it was best if he was left alone for a while.

He went out to the stables; something about being around the gentle horses calmed him down.

As he ran his hand down the flank of his chestnut brown mare, he trembled with anger and hatred toward his father. "How dare he threaten me!" William snapped. Averia nickered softly as if to comfort him. "And you know what really makes me angry? The fact that after all these years of getting what he wants, he *still* isn't satisfied! When is it going to be enough?"

Averia put her head against William's shoulder, nickering again.

"Yes, you are right, as always," William said to the gentle mare. "He'll never have enough."

"Just leave me here please, Thomas, and I'll be ready to go as soon as you're finished with your business."

Anna dismounted her horse and watched as Thomas briskly rode away. She securely tied her horse to the hitching post, then walked a ways until she came to the place she had been looking for.

She walked up the few stairs of the little white church and opened the door. Stepping inside, her heart was filled with true joy again. Just being in the house of the Lord brought Anna such peace.

How she missed those peaceful Sundays, her favorite day of the week.

Anna surveyed the long wooden benches facing the podium in the front of the church. Her breath was taken away as she noticed the beautiful stained glass window.

Jesus was ascending into the heavens on a pure white cloud. Around Him hovered four white angels, their heads bowed in reverence to their King. Below Him knelt His disciples. A bright light as strong as the sun surrounded them all.

Anna thought of how gloriously sad that day must have been for them—to lose such a precious Friend, but to witness such an amazing event.

"May I help you, Miss?" a kind voice asked, startling Anna out of her thoughts.

Anna spun around and was greeted by a pleasant-faced man. She offered him a slight curtsy and gave him a smile. "I'm Anna Haddington," she said, holding her hand out to the kind-faced man, who looked oddly familiar.

He took it and shook it heartily. "And I am Reverend Mattheus," he spoke, a smile lighting up his countenance. "Can I do anything for you?"

Anna nodded, her brow crinkling. "Were you the man at the ticket station? The one who told me of my aunt's death?"

Mattheus nodded. "Indeed I am. So we meet again, my dear. I've prayed for you daily and I'm sorry for leaving so abruptly. There was a death among the flock and I needed to offer comfort to the grieving."

Anna smiled slightly. "That's quite alright, sir. Actually, I was feeling quite sorry for you. The people at the station didn't seem to take very kindly to you for some reason."

Mattheus chuckled, the sound was full of warmth and reminded Anna of her father. "No, they think I run their business off by praying for them every day. But, you didn't come here to listen to me talk about myself, what can I do for you?"

"I'm looking for a Bible for a dear friend of mine," Anna began. "I know they are rather hard to come by, but I thought a church would be the best place to look."

"You are correct about that, Miss Anna. And do you yourself own a Bible?"

"It is my most precious possession, sir," Anna said sincerely.

"I wish more people had your conviction, my dear," Mattheus shook his head sadly. "Would you care to sit down?"

Anna answered that she would, and he led the way to one of the wooden pews toward the front of the church. She slid into a pew and he sat down directly in front of her.

"Tell me a little of yourself," he questioned.

"I came here to live with my aunt after I lost my mother and father," Anna began, though he already knew that much.

"Jane Willowbee," he stated, his eyes saddening.

Anna's expression grew somber. "Did you know her well?"

"Yes, dear. And you look a little like her as well. You have the same gentle smile and joy-filled eyes," he replied.

"She was very active in this church and she and I were the best of friends. I don't think there lives a soul within one hundred miles who doesn't know Jane's story." When he saw Anna's look of confusion, he spoke again. His voice was gentle as he continued. "You don't know how your aunt died, do you?"

"I never knew who to ask," Anna said truthfully.

"Your aunt was killed for her faith." Mattheus' eyes took on a faraway look as he thought back to the devastating day....

"Jane Willowbee," an armed guard stood beside her cell, watching her intently, "you have one last chance to renounce your faith."
He patiently awaited her response, but he didn't need to wait for long. Jane's response was quick, spoken with strong conviction and easy to understand.

"Never."

The guard sighed; it seemed to come from deep within his soul. "Very well." He turned to leave, but Jane stopped him.

"Stephen," she said softly.

The guard froze—he was caught. He had been a fool to believe his armed disguise would keep him from being recognized. Slowly, he turned around, his face masked by a look of stone, but underneath it, Jane knew he was suffering.

"I am not afraid of dying," she spoke, her voice wavering with emotion. "I am not afraid of what man can do to me. The worst man could possibly do is destroy my body. I fear Him who cannot only destroy both body and soul, but cast them into the lake of fire, to live in torment forever. I'm not leaving my home, Stephen, I'm going there!" Jane's voice broke as she placed a hand on top of Stephen's. "I am going to a place where there is no more sorrow and no more pain. The place my Father has prepared for me, and it was *His* choice, not yours, nor the king's, but *His* choice to summon me there." She paused. "That is why," she whispered, "I couldn't possibly renounce my faith."

Stephen looked at her, his eyes bright with unshed tears.

"I pray for you, Stephen," Jane went on. "You can have salvation too! You can be saved from the

Day of Judgment that is coming, if only you repent of your sins and turn from your wicked ways."

Stephen grabbed onto the bars of her cell. "You know I can't, Mother! I have no choice!" Stephen's shoulders trembled as he sobbed, and he quickly turned, fleeing from the dark dungeon.

"Oh, but you do, my son," Jane whispered, tears streaming down her face, "you do."

Anna brushed her tears away. "I had no idea," she murmured quietly. "Poor Auntie, and how awful Stephen must have felt. How did he get there in the first place?"

"He was chosen by the king to become a guard at the palace," Mattheus answered. "It was an honored position, but he never knew he would be commanded to sentence his own mother to death. Stephen was a tender-hearted lad before he left, but he was not saved and his heart was easily led astray.

"The king ruined him by polluting his heart and mind, and then used poor Stephen in his evil schemes."

"But how did my aunt get to be in that position?" Anna asked.

"She came every day to speak with Stephen and implore him to leave. Once she heard of the many things the king stood for, she didn't want her son near him. One day the king heard her praying as she waited to meet with Stephen. In his anger, he commanded Jane to never come near the castle again. Well, she stayed away only for a few days, but her motherly heart and her lack of fear for man soon brought her back. When the king found her again, he commanded her to be taken away because she had disobeyed his command."

"Did he have any other reason for killing her?" Anna asked him quietly.

"She was a follower of Christ and, for him, that was reason enough. The king is ruthless, and he will stop at nothing to see that those who follow Christ are diminished. Strangely though, he doesn't seem to seek us out. If he did, we'd have all died a long time ago. He seems to strike at the ones who get in his way—the ones consistently reminding him of the Lord. I pray for his salvation daily; he has such a wicked heart. None of us are without sin, but he has just chosen to embrace his."

"But he seemed so kind when I first met him," Anna mused, almost to herself.

Mattheus's face showed clear surprise. "You have met the king?" he inquired.

"I... I work for him, sir," Anna answered hesitantly.

She saw an indiscernible look spread over Mattheus's face.

"You know the price you might pay for that?"

Anna was quiet as she thought of his question. She *did* know. She knew only too well what would happen.

"The king will try to kill you if he finds out you are a follower of Christ." Mattheus continued.

Anna's bright eyes were filled with conviction. "I am not afraid of dying for my faith, sir," she answered evenly.

"I know," Mattheus replied. "I figured as much already."

"How did my aunt die?" Anna asked, her voice trembling with emotion.

Mattheus knew exactly what she meant. "With the faith of a child," he replied. "Her voice lifted to her Creator with praise and thanksgiving. And with the joy of a believer, making her way into paradise."

The sight of Thomas quickly riding down the dusty road told Anna her time with Mattheus was growing short.

"Thank you so much!" Anna spoke, as she shook Mattheus' hand.

In her hands, she held a black leather-bound Bible.

She walked down the rickety steps of the old church and turned to wave at him. "I shall do what you suggested, Reverend," Anna said with a smile as Thomas came riding up to them.

She walked toward her horse and mounted him, the Bible hidden well beneath her cloak.

Thomas's eyebrows rose as he looked at Anna and back to the little white church. The reverend was nowhere in sight.

Anna noticed his questioning stare, but decided to keep quiet.

After a few moments of silence, Anna tried to think of a way to tell Thomas what was on her mind.

"You know, Thomas," Anna began. "As servants and maids of our king, well, we're all in this together, right?" Anna wanted to make sure no words were spoken concerning her visit with Mattheus.

Thomas's dark face was lit by a smile as he nodded. "I's know what you tryin' to say, child."

Anna looked at him in surprise. "You do?"

Thomas turned in the saddle and faced her. "I's might not have had me much education, and I's might have pretty butchered English, but Thomas here's got a nice head on his shoulders."

Anna couldn't help but laugh at his comment. At first, Thomas just smiled, but Anna's laughing was contagious, and soon he was laughing as well.

Anna had forgotten how good that felt. Solomon sure knew what he was talking about when he wrote in the Bible that laughter was good medicine.

As they headed over the mountain, they stopped at the top of the hill overlooking the castle and village below.

Anna took a deep breath, relishing the sweet moments of freedom she had been granted.

They broke their horses into a trot and soon entered the village.

As they passed through the palace gate, Anna thought she saw movement in the bushes. Thomas noticed too, and they both slowed their horses down as they rounded the bend to the stables.

Anna's heart raced as she thought of all the things she had just learned about the king. She took a deep breath, willing her heart to slow down. As she unsaddled her horse and put him out to graze, she murmured aloud a verse in John:

"These things I have spoken unto you, that in me ye might have peace. In the world ye shall have tribulation: but be of good cheer; I have overcome the world."

She turned and walked briskly toward the back door of the kitchen, her body and mind filled with newfound peace. She tucked the Bible further beneath her maroon cloak and stopped before the door.

"Whatever happens," Anna whispered to herself. "I won't ever stop being *His*."

Thirteen

"Now that you've given your life to Christ," Caleb began, "you are a new creation."

Caleb and Amira sat side by side on a branch of a mighty oak tree, overlooking the silvery lake.

After Amira's visit with Caleb's pastor, she had given her life to Christ. Caleb had noticed a huge difference in her already.

"A new creation?" Amira repeated, wrinkling her brow in confusion.

"Yes," Caleb replied with a smile. "It means you are a new person, and that you have put your old self behind you. The Amira who used to *not* believe in Jesus, now believes in Him. That is your *new* self! Does that make sense?"

Amira was silent for a moment. "Yes, I think so."

Caleb looked at her seriously. "Have you told your papa and maman yet?" he asked, concern filling his voice.

Amira's dark brown eyes filled with tears and she grasped the tree branch, her knuckles turning white. "No," she replied, her voice no louder than a whisper. She looked at Caleb with a look he would never forget. "Must I?"

Caleb was silent for a moment, thinking of what he would do if he were in her place. But it was too horrible for him to imagine. She could be thrown out into the streets if her parents heard of her confession of faith, or worse. Caleb shuddered despite the warm afternoon. He looked back at Amira, aware that she was still waiting for his answer.

"No," Caleb replied. "I don't think you must tell them, at least, not yet."

He noticed Amira's body relax. They both stared out over the lake, lost in their own thoughts. Caleb knew Amira needed to get out of the mosque. It was the right thing to do now that she was saved. It was going to take an awfully big leap of faith. But faith, he knew, was growing inside of his lifelong friend.

His thoughts were interrupted by Amira's voice, which had already gained back some of its cheerfulness. "I better head home."

Caleb jumped down from the tree branch, Amira following close at his heels.

As they walked the short distance home, Caleb brought up the subject pressing heavily upon his mind. "Amira," he started, "you must not go to your mosque any longer."

He shouldn't have been surprised by her answer, but for some reason, he was.

"I know," she said. Her tone was dead. "God will grant me the faith to do what needs to be done." Her voice began to grow with conviction, "I am not afraid of dying for my faith." They crossed the bridge, stopping in the middle. "I know that whatever happens, everything is going to be alright," she told him.

"And I shall be praying for you, Amira," Caleb promised.

"Thanks, Caleb," she said, smiling up at him.

They went their separate ways at the edge of the bridge and as Caleb headed home, he thought of how strong Amira's faith was already.

Was he ready to die for his faith? Would he have the courage to do the right thing?

He stuck his hand in his pocket and pulled it out in surprise.

Anna's letter! He had forgotten all about it. Everything in him ached to tear into it and read its contents. But he knew he must wait to share it with his sisters.

Margret and Julianna would be so pleased to hear from Anna.

Well, he must wait and that was that.

He began to pray for Amira and the trials he knew were about to come her way.

He prayed without ceasing, all through the rest of his chores, all through supper and all through the evening, until his head touched his pillow and his eyes closed in sleep.

Stephen closed his eyes, willing his body to sleep. But it wouldn't come. It hadn't come. Not since that dreadful night buried deep within his memory.

He had been a part of a wicked plan that killed his own mother. *She wasn't my birth mother,* he argued stubbornly.

Before she had taken him in, he had lived on the streets. But he had betrayed her and all the love and kindness she had shown him.

He had hoped his cropped hair and clean-shaven face accompanied by his suit of armor would keep her from realizing it was him. But of course that hadn't fooled her. He shuddered at the memory.

The look in her eyes haunted him every day since. It wasn't a look of helplessness, or anger, or even fright. It was a look of pure peace, and of love for him, as well as anguish that he had chosen such an awful path.

Stephen slung his legs over the side of his bed and walked over to the window, brushing the curtain aside.

The window overlooked the grand palace lawn and its beauty would have been breathtaking, if he only took the time to notice.

One would think that after being part of such an event, Stephen would have done everything within his power to flee from the king and his evil ways.

But the king had offered too much for his youthful mind to throw away; wealth beyond compare, if only he would stay as long as he was needed.

But he was growing tired of the way he had been living and wished for peace to come. He would leave right now, if he had a place to go. He had nowhere to turn. But was that the true reason he didn't leave? Or was his love of money keeping him here?

A sigh escaped his lips as he turned from the window and sat back down on his bed.

There was no hope for him anymore. No forgiveness could possibly be granted from the God his mother believed in. He had gone too far this time; there was no other choice but to stay in the life he had chosen and to wait until death brought him the peace he longed for.

If only Stephen knew that the peace he was longing for was just within his reach. And if only he knew of the battle that would take place within his very soul.

William securely locked his door before heading off to bed. He hated living in fear, but he couldn't be certain of what his father had in mind.

Just as he closed his eyes, he was interrupted by a knock at his door. His brow furrowed in confusion as he went to answer it.

He walked past a small table by his bedside and grabbed a silver candlestick.

He silently placed his hand on the door, unlocking it and opening it slowly. His left hand held the candlestick high, ready to strike.

The king knew he had made a terrible mistake, speaking to William the way he did. How was he ever going to carry out his plans without William's help?

He quickly called Ahmad and told him of his plight. Ahmad was hesitant in offering his suggestion until he saw that the king was quickly becoming impatient.

"You—you could apologize to Prince William... Your Majesty," Ahmad stuttered.

The king's face gradually grew redder and redder as he listened.

Ahmad braced himself for the outburst he knew was about to come.

"*Apologize?*" the king raged, his face burning with embarrassment. He grabbed Ahmad's shirt in his rugged hand, pulling the guard's face close to his. "And what, pray tell, do I have to apologize for?"

The king's eyes seemed to bore into Ahmad's very soul, and it took all that was in him to return the steady gaze. "Why, nothing, Your Majesty." His voice sounded stronger than he felt inside. "I only thought—" Ahmad began.

"Maybe that's your problem," the king interrupted. He let go of Ahmad's shirt and turned his back to him. He quickly spun around and motioned Ahmad out the room. "Get out of my sight, you fool!" he spat.

Ahmad turned quickly on his heel and fled, desperate not to anger the king any further.

As Ahmad's steps retreated, the king sat on a window seat made of oak, lined with deep red velvet.

But his mind wandered far beyond the walls of his luxurious room.

"I shall go and apologize," he spoke aloud. "Of course, I have nothing to apologize for, but I shall pretend I am sorry, and then everything will go back to normal, and he will be a part of my plans."

He quickly left his seat and found his way to William's room, but when he tried to open the door, it was locked.

A scowl covered the king's face, but he quickly replaced it with a false smile.

William was not sure who was more surprised, himself or his father. But if his father had been surprised, he quickly recovered.

"Father?" William asked, his voice shocked.

"William, my son." The king smiled at him. "I came to offer my deep regrets for my behavior a while ago."

William looked at his father in confusion, noticing he was waiting for his response. He slowly lowered the candle stick. "Alright," he said slowly, still unaware of what his father had in mind.

"Good," the king said, a smile still frozen on his face.

William stood silent, having no possible clue as to what to say.

Finally, the king turned on his heel and walked away.

William closed the door on the bewildering scene.

He leaned against his door, letting out a sigh of confusion. Slowly, he shook his head, trying to clear his mind.

Right now he was too exhausted to try to sort it all out. He looked down at his hand and noticed he was still holding the silver candlestick.

"A lot of help that would have done if I truly were in danger!" He laughed scornfully.

All he wanted right now, was to rest. He lay his tired body down on his bed for the second time that night and soon drifted off to sleep.

Anna felt joyously happy as she cradled her new possession close to her body.

It was almost midnight, the time she and Grandmother had appointed for their visit.

As she silently walked up the staircase, she smiled inwardly at how happy Grandmother would be with her gift.

When she reached Grandmother's room, she quietly listened for their secret sign. A soft meowing reached Anna's ears; she opened the door and quietly slipped in.

Grandmother sat in her window seat with plush pillows lining her frail body.

A smile as bright as the sun illuminated her aging features.

"Where is the cat?" Anna asked, playing along, as she quickly walked over to her friend.

"Anna, my dear!" Agnes cried in delight. "I thought you would never come!"

Anna grasped the lady's thin hand in her own and smiled. "One would think you had a real cat in your room."

"Oh, but I do," replied Agnes, in mock defense. They both burst out laughing. Anna covered her mouth with her hand, in an effort to muffle the sound.

"Can I see it?" Anna asked, her eyes twinkling. But she didn't wait for an answer. "Look what I brought you!" Anna exclaimed as she presented the black Bible she had gotten from Mattheus.

Tears filled Agnes' eyes as she thanked Anna again and again for the precious gift. "I shall treasure it always!" she responded. She gave Anna a hug and told her she had never been given such a precious gift before.

She sat down next to Agnes, deciding that this was the right time to ask her about the hidden bookshelf. "Do you... know anything about a hidden shelf in the library?" Anna asked hesitantly.

Agnes' head shot up from the Bible that she had already started flipping through. "How do you know about that?" Agnes snapped. Anna's face filled with momentary shock.

Agnes' voice was gentle as she apologized. "I'm sorry, I didn't mean for my words to come out so harshly. Would you please forgive me, dear?"

"Of course," Anna stammered. "It's none of my business."

"No," replied Agnes, "I do believe it is, and I think it's time for someone else to be told the story."

Anna's brow knit in confusion. "What story?" she asked, her interest piqued.

"The story of my daughter-in-law and her husband. The king and the late queen of Carpathia...."

The sun poured down brightly on Isabelle, but her heart and mind were far from the weather.

She was getting married, and to the king himself! Well, he wasn't the king yet, but knowing how his poor father was ailing, it wouldn't be long. She couldn't believe it; the daughter of a lighthouse keeper was going to be married to the soon-to-be king!

Her mother's voice brought her out of her thoughts.

"Isabelle, dear! Come try on your wedding dress!"

Isabelle ran along the path from her flower garden to the house.

She stepped onto the threshold of their small cottage and gave her mother a gentle hug. Her mother caught Isabelle's face between her hands and kissed her forehead. "My own daughter! To be queen!"

With one more kiss, she led Isabelle to the almost-finished wedding dress and bid her to try it on.

"Oh, it's beautiful, Mother!" Isabelle cried in delight.

"Hurry," her mother said with a smile, "I'm anxious to see it on you!"

Mother and daughter worked for the rest of the day on the silky white gown. The wedding day dawned bright and clear, and Raymond and Isabelle were happily married—

"That nice, sweet girl married the dreadful king?" Anna interrupted. Then it hit her that she was talking to the dreadful king's *mother.* "I didn't mean—" she whispered, flustered.

"It's alright," Agnes sighed. "You see, my son hasn't always been as awful as he is today. He was much different before. A tender-hearted young man devoted to his new wife and his newly acquired kingship. It wasn't even a year after they had married that they had my grandson. But I'm getting ahead of myself...."

Isabelle smiled up at her husband, her eyes filled with pure happiness. "It's a boy!" she whispered softly. "You have a son!"

Raymond tenderly took the precious bundle in his strong arms and looked at him with delight. "I have a son." He laughed. "I have a son!"

The baby let out a piercing wail, and both mother and father smiled. Raymond placed the baby boy gently back in his mother's arms.

"What shall we name him?" she asked.

"William," Raymond said, "after your Father."

"And Raymond, after yours," Isabelle insisted. She looked at her precious baby and smiled. "William Raymond," she said slowly, savoring each word. "I think that suits you quite nicely, don't you?"

William's blue eyes opened wide as he wrapped his tiny hand around his mother's finger.

"My poor daughter-in-law was never the same after she gave birth to William," Agnes said sadly. "The doctors never knew what went wrong, why she was often so sickly. But she never gained her strength back after he was born, and when she had her little daughter, it took all the life she had left.

Little William was only six. She was so young," Agnes murmured, half to herself. "And even until death her only thoughts were for her husband and children...."

"Raymond?" Isabelle feebly cried out.

"I'm here," Raymond's voice was filled with emotion and he didn't trust himself to say more.

"I want you to promise me you will teach our children the ways of the Lord when I am gone," she requested softly.

"You're not going anywhere!" Raymond said with conviction, taking Isabelle's hand in his own.

"We have neglected teaching our son the ways of God, and he needs to know the precious story of redemption!"

Raymond promised he would.

"I'm only going home a little while before you, my husband," she went on. "No longer will I be here on this earth where sorrow and pain fill my days. And I shall be waiting for you," she said softly. Her breath came in short gasps and her face turned even whiter against the pillow.

Raymond tightly clamped his jaw and tried to keep his emotions at bay. But it wasn't to be; tears slid down his face as he listened to his wife's last words.

"Please sing to me the beautiful words once again," she requested, her voice no louder than a whisper.

He took a deep breath, his voice still quivering with emotion, and began to sing:

Jesus, lover of my soul,
Let me to Thy bosom fly,
While the nearer waters roll,
While the tempest still is high.
Hide me, O my Savior, hide,
Till the storm of life is past;
Safe into the haven guide;
Oh, receive my soul at last.

He was quiet as he listened to her breathing.

When he was certain she had fallen asleep, he walked quietly over to the pink cradle sitting at the foot of his bed. He gazed with hatred at the little form, sleeping so peacefully in her cradle. "You are the one who has caused me all this pain," he whispered harshly. A soft moaning from the bed brought him back to his wife's side.

Isabelle tightly clasped his hand as she gasped for breath. She looked up at her husband's face, beckoning him to come closer.

"Show our children love," she murmured.

Her words were so quiet, Raymond had to lean close to hear them.

A peaceful smile lit Isabella's face and her hand went limp in his.

Sobs shook Raymond's body and he hid his face in his hands, a face that seemed to have aged ten years in mere seconds.

He never slept that night, and when morning came, he had determined to put God behind him in his life.

"He never wanted to have anything to do with us or He wouldn't have let my wife die!" he declared angrily. He had commanded Isabelle never to teach William about those fables from a useless Book. He should have instructed her to stay away from them as well.

He commanded the next servant he saw. "Take every Bible and Christian literature in this castle and burn them!" he ordered.

The servant hesitated. "Excuse me, Your Majesty?" The servant's eyes were filled with confusion.

"Just do what I say and don't let me ever hear you, or anyone else, mention the Lord's name in this palace ever again!"

The servant quickly went to do as he was told, terribly confused at the sudden change that had come over his master.

"I had been traveling in France for almost a year, and I returned only the day before Isabelle's death." Agnes brushed at a tear that had slowly found its way down her cheek. "The baby girl died only three days after she was born."

"How did all the Bibles and other literature get into the secret shelf?" Anna asked, the question weighing heavily on her mind.

"When I overheard Raymond's command, I didn't think he really meant it. I thought he would come around and regret burning his wife's favorite possessions, so I quickly gathered up most of the precious books and had the shelf crafted by a friend of mine one day when Raymond was out on business."

"The Bible I saw," Anna said with a sad smile, "that must have been Isabelle's Bible."

"Yes," replied Agnes, "but, my, that was almost twelve years ago," she mused aloud.

Anna looked out of the window at the silvery moon. "It shows you what years without Christ will do to a soul."

Agnes knew only too well the truth of that statement.

As Anna prepared for bed that evening—or rather, morning, for it was almost three o'clock—she couldn't help but sympathize with the king. And her pity for William only grew.

She began to see the life this royal family had been living from a different perspective.

She hoped, with God's help, that she would be able to change that perspective.

Fourteen

Anna positioned the heavy load of laundry on her hip as she went from room to room, collecting the soiled garments.

She had felt nothing but pity for Stephen since she'd heard his saddening story. She wondered if he had forgiven himself for the awful deed. She also wondered if he had asked God to forgive him as well.

I must find him, she thought.

She dumped the laundry into a bigger basket that would be taken out to wash in a few hours, once the sun came up.

Anna woke at four every morning so that she would have time for her daily Bible reading before she became busy with her day.

No one else was up at that hour, and it seemed the wise thing to do.

She walked into the kitchen and was greeted by Lilly and her mother, who, before she walked in, must have been enjoying a lively conversation. But as soon as she stepped into the kitchen, their voices were hushed; only the crackling of the fire in the stove could be heard.

Anna pretended not to notice as she went to grab a pile of torn rags to wash the floor.

Lilly whispered something to her mother, Josie, and Josie replied in the same tone. Josie glanced at Anna and sadly shook her head. Lilly looked as if she were trying very hard not to cry.

Anna's heart began to beat faster as she realized that they must have been talking about her.

As Josie started walking toward her, she tried to calm herself, but to no avail. "Anna," she whispered. "Ya've been a friend to us, helpin' us out with money and all to get me the proper medicine I's needed."

Anna looked at her in surprise. "I never mentioned anything about it, how did you know it was me?"

Josie's eyes softened. "Who else would it be, child? I've not done seen so much kindness since before the Queen herself died. It's 'cause of that, I feel I should warn ya."

Without thinking, Anna took a step back. "Warn me of what?"

"Warn ya ta guard that mouth of yourn from what ya been sayin'."

Anna knew, without asking, what Josie meant. She also knew it was an impossible request to fulfill. "I can't ever stop talking about the Lord and the work He has done and is doing in me," she responded.

Josie's eyebrows shot up in surprise. "Then ya must not be lovin' your own life!" her voice was still scarcely above a whisper.

"I think I tend to love my life more than I ought to," Anna replied. "But it is because I love my Savior and the work He has done in me that I cannot keep from sharing His story. There is a day of judgment that is coming, Josie, and I can't keep silent about it."

Josie looked at Anna with pity. Without another word, she briskly walked away.

Anna's heart went out to the poor woman, and she told herself that she must pray diligently for Josie's salvation. Anna continued to work on the floor in silence, praying for Josie's heart to be softened.

She was startled when she looked up and found Lilly standing near.

There were tears on the child's face and Anna could tell that something weighed heavily on Lilly's mind.

"What's the matter, Lilly?" Anna inquired, her voice filled with concern.

"I must be tellin' ya somthin'," Lilly sobbed, tears streaming down her face. "That day when Momma was so ill, I prayed God would go an' send some way to be helpin' her. He heard my prayers 'cause he sent the money." Lilly's voice was thick with tears as she went on, "That day I prayed and asked the Lord to save me from that day of judgment you was talking about. I've done felt somthin' different in me since that day, but I's been too scared to talk with anyone 'bout it."

Tears filled Anna's eyes as she opened her arms to Lilly.

Lilly gladly went into them. Sobs shook her thin frame as Anna went on to tell her how happy she was to hear the words she had just spoken.

"Now there are three lights in this old palace," Anna whispered softly.

At Lilly's look of confusion, Anna laughed quietly. "I'll explain it at another time." A few minutes later as they worked side by side on the kitchen floor, Anna told her, "I can't tell you how earnestly I have prayed to see this day."

A smile as bright as the sun itself lit Lilly's brown face. "Momma just cares for ya, thet's all."

Anna set her rag down and stood up, not taking her eyes off Lilly. "I know, but you understand now why I can't just keep it to myself, right?"

It took a while for Lilly to answer but finally she nodded her head slowly. "I think so."

Betty walked into the kitchen at that time, ceasing any more talk that may have happened in her absence.

Anna was soon needed to chop vegetables for dinner.

She carried the heavy load of water outside, thinking how funny her sisters would think it was, that she started dinner preparations even before they had eaten breakfast!

Lilly felt very brave after talking with Anna about her faith and decided to broach the subject with Betty.

They were alone, as Anna had just stepped outside, so she took a deep breath and began. "Guess what, Betty?" Lilly asked, her eyes shining with excitement.

"What, child?" She sighed, quite preoccupied in slicing fresh-roasted peacock into pieces for a pie.

"I done and gave my life to Christ and now I'm saved!" Excitement shone in Lilly's eyes.

Betty spun around, dropping her knife in her haste.

"What'd ya say, child?" she almost yelled.

Lilly took a step back, her face filled with alarm. "I...I said I gave my life ta Christ," she went on bravely.

Lilly cried out in pain as Betty grabbed her arm tightly.

"What'd ya think yar doing, child? If the king hears of this, you'll be killed afore the sun goes down!"

Lilly's small body was trembling, but somehow she found the courage to speak again. "Anna said that—"

"That Anna girl is nothin' but a scullery maid and she needs to learn ta be keepin' that mouth shut!" Betty turned around, stooping to pick up her knife and began chopping with renewed vigor. "She's gonna be killed someday, just like that old aunt of hers, and it's gonna serve her right, too!"

Fear filled Lilly's eyes as she slowly backed away. Spinning around, she ran out the kitchen door and away from the frightening scene.

Betty's face filled with anger. "I'm gonna do somthin' about that Anna girl, ya I am," she resolved. "Our life was just fine 'til she up and came into it, and I'm gonna be doin' somthin' 'bout it, that I will!"

William walked briskly up the garden path, willing his nerves to relax.

He had just overheard his father speaking with Ahmad, and it didn't sound good.

He had heard things like, *over with* and *after it's done*. He thought he heard him mention something about a dungeon too, but he hoped he had just imagined that part. He never heard them mention Anna's name, and he hoped with all his being she was not the subject of their conversation.

But something deep within himself told him that she was exactly who they were speaking of.

William stopped short when he thought he heard someone crying. He followed the sound until he came to a clearing about twenty feet away. He hid behind a row of bushes and tried to find out what was going on.

Looking on in curiosity, he watched as Anna knelt down before the sobbing girl and took her in her arms, hugging her gently and rocking them back and forth.

He strained to listen as Anna began speaking.

"Now, can you tell me what happened?" Anna asked gently, leaning back so she could see Lilly's face.

Between sobs, Lilly told her all that had passed between Betty and her in the kitchen. "I ain't very strong ta cry so much," she finished.

"I don't think crying has anything to do with being strong or not," Anna told her. "Even I cry sometimes. I think you were very brave to share your faith with Betty like that, and I wouldn't pay her comments any mind." Anna smiled sweetly and Lilly felt much better.

"Ya mean that nothin' will happen to ya?" she asked.

"No, I can't say that, but only God knows what shall happen to us day unto day, and He has told us in His Word that it is a sin to worry over it."

Lilly's face filled with shock. "Has He?"

"Yes," Anna replied. "Would you like to know a secret?" excitement brightened her eyes.

Lilly nodded, a small smile lifting the corners of her mouth.

"Grandmother...I mean, Agnes and I, meet every other night and go over the Scriptures. Would you like to join us?"

Lilly's face filled with delight as she nodded again.

Anna told her what time to meet, and then they both stood up, walking back to the palace kitchen and admiring the flowers as they went.

Lilly was not at a loss for words as they headed back to the palace kitchen, and Anna was truly blessed at the change in her little friend. As they headed back to work, a new spring was in Anna's step. She had gained the confidence of her little friend, and it was such a blessing, truly, that one more light now brightened up this dark and dismal palace.

William was not only shocked at Anna's words, but slightly hurt that Grandmother had not told him that she had been meeting with Anna.

He could have guessed. He had already suspected as much, but he would have felt better hearing it from his grandmother first.

William had much to think about as he walked through the palace doors.

He was so wrapped up in his thoughts that he didn't think of waiting to be let in, but rather opened the door and let himself in—much to the dismay of the servant standing directly behind it.

The servant was so shocked at the prince's odd behavior, that he froze, staring at William's retreating back.

He stood there until another maid finally walked by and set him in his place.

"Shut the door, James, you're letting the flies in!" she snapped.

Out of habit, James did as he was told.

The king was more than ready to carry out his plot, and, with Ahmad's help, that's exactly what he planned to do. He was resting on his bed, thinking of how clever he was to think of such a good tactic.

A quick knock brought him to his feet. A servant opened his door and let him know that Ahmad was waiting to see him.

"Send him in!" he yelled impatiently.

Ahmad quickly walked in without a moment's hesitation.

"Well?" the king questioned him.

"We have reason to believe, Your Majesty," Ahmad started, "that the new scullery maid is indeed a follower of Christ." Ahmad stared down at his feet. He took a deep breath and continued. "I watched her return from the city with Thomas, and she was carrying a book that looked to be a copy of the Bible." The king's eyes lit up joyously as he commanded Ahmad to continue. "And she's been speaking openly about Christ with the other servants," Ahmad finished solemnly.

The king laughed happily and clapped his hands, then rubbed them together. Looking Ahmad in the eye he spoke. "You know what to do next."

Ahmad left the room, the king's laugh sending chills up his spine. He now thoroughly hated his job as second hand of the king.

Innocent people were going to get hurt, and he was forced to be a part of it.

Fifteen

Lilly, feeling quite recovered from her episode yesterday, had been looking forward to her first 'real study,' as she had been calling it.

Tonight, she would meet with Anna and Agnes and go over the Scriptures. Her heart sang with joy as she ran into the little cabin she called home.

It was late afternoon, and the sun cast its eerie shadows around the room. She let her eyes adjust to the darkness and walked cautiously over to her mat by the wall. She would wait until her mother went to sleep and then she would leave at ten to midnight. That would give her plenty of time to get to the kitchen. From there, she and Anna would go up the spiral staircase to Grandmother's room.

She looked up as her mother entered the cabin. She watched as Josie quickly lit a lantern and set it on a nearby table. Lilly sat there silently, watching her every move, sensing that something was amiss.

Her mother sat down heavily in a wicker rocking chair, motioning for Lilly to come near.

Lilly came slowly, her eyes glued to the floor. "I've did somthin' wrong, ain't that right?" Lilly asked.

"No, child, I's been hopin' it ain't true," her mother answered. "Did ya go and tell Anna and Betty that ya gave yar life to Christ?" Josie asked. Lilly was silent. "Well, did ya?" Josie persisted.

Lilly looked at her mother evenly and answered her, her voice sounding stronger than she felt. "Ya, Momma, I did."

"Then it's true, ain't it?" Josie groaned.

"I'm saved, Momma," Lilly spoke softly. "And it be 'cause of Anna and her teachin' me!" Lilly's face lit up as she spoke. "And I must be tellin'—"

"You won't be telling any others, child!" Josie told her sharply, grabbing Lilly by the shoulders and giving them a slight shake. "If ya value ya own life, you'll keep quiet 'bout it!" Josie's voice was hard and strained.

"Don't ya believe in Him, Momma?" Lilly asked, her voice quivering slightly.

Josie didn't answer for the longest time. When she did answer, her voice was dead. "Yes, child." She embraced Lilly and held her tight. Tears filled her eyes as she tried to gain enough control to speak.

"But I can't bear to lose another child." Sobs shook Josie's body as her grasp tightened around Lilly.

She thanked the Lord for her two daughters, still close enough to embrace.

Lilly's quiet footsteps seemed to echo through the cabin.

Her heart was pounding so loudly within her chest that she was afraid it would wake her mother.

The talk with her mother a few hours before had only strengthened her resolve to join Anna and Agnes in their study tonight. She wanted to learn how to be the best daughter she could to her precious mother.

As she opened the door slowly, she stopped, holding her breath as her mother turned over in her sleep. Lilly waited until her breathing became steady again, then she slipped silently out the door and into the starry night.

Stephen had been quietly observing Anna since her arrival at the palace.

Something was different about her, something he couldn't quite make sense of. But for some reason, she reminded him of his own mother.

She seemed to be happy here, a place filled with darkness and depression. And everywhere she went, she brought light with her.

He wanted what she had, the peacefulness that surrounded her.

You know you're too far gone for that, the tempter whispered.

But every one of us deserves a second chance, his conscience whispered back.

There's no use in even trying, the tempter continued.

But think of the joy and peace you would gain from this heavy burden being lifted from your shoulders.

Stephen grabbed his head and let out a groan. "Stop it!" he growled to himself. "I shall speak with Anna. I can't go on living like this any longer! I'll speak with her tomorrow."

He hoped with all that was in him that it wasn't too late.

Lilly walked slowly to the palace kitchen, savoring the tranquility of the peaceful night.

Now she could actually say that her own Father created all this! A smile lit her face as she walked through the courtyard and around the back of the palace. She was just about to step inside, when a hand suddenly grabbed her from behind.

She let out a scream, but it was muffled by a strong hand covering her mouth.

Her breathing became rapid, her body going limp with fear.

"You mustn't be afraid, Lilly," her captor whispered. "It is I, Prince William."

Lilly turned around, a look of terror upon her face. William crouched down to her level, a look of sympathy covering his features.

"I hadn't meant to startle you," he apologized. His voice was still low.

"What do ya want with me, Your Majesty?" Lilly questioned. Her voice still held a bit of fear, but her face was slowly regaining its color.

"I don't want you to meet with Anna and Grandmother tonight," he told her. Seeing Lilly's disappointment, he was suddenly afraid she would go anyway. "Anna is in grave danger," he went on. "It would only make matters worse if you went on with your plans." He hadn't wanted to tell her that much, but he feared it was his only choice.

Lilly thought about his words. Could the prince be trusted? She had heard things about the king, and she had seen his cruelty with her own eyes. But was Prince William different than him? Real fear dawned in Lilly's face as she began to understand. "Will Anna be alright?" she asked, her tone edged with worry.

"I'm going to do everything within my power to make it so," he promised.

Lilly's small arms encircled William's neck, catching him off guard. But he quickly composed himself, awkwardly patting her back.

"Now you must get back to bed," he told her kindly.

Lilly smiled at him, and William watched as she retraced her steps. He waited until he was sure that she was safely back at her cabin.

Then he walked up to the kitchen door, and deftly stepped inside.

Anna was waiting patiently for Lilly, but when she heard the clock strike twelve-thirty, she was afraid Lilly had changed her mind. She hoped nothing serious had happened.

She was just about to give up and leave without her when the kitchen door leading outside opened slowly.

The figure that stepped inside was the opposite of Lilly's thin frame. Anna's heart leapt to her throat as she took a step back in fear.

Lord, please protect me! she prayed silently.

Mustering up enough courage, she cried out softly, "Who's there?"

William hadn't meant to startle Lilly, and he definitely hadn't meant to startle Anna, but he seemed to have a knack for it this evening.

He jumped back in fear as her quiet voice rang out into the darkness of the kitchen. His hand bumped against a pile of dishes which fell to the ground with a sickening clang. He sucked in his breath, trying to regain his composure, hoping that no one else had heard the noise.

"It's me, William," he whispered loudly.

Anna lit a small candle, illuminating the kitchen with a soft glow of light. "What are you doing here, Your Majesty?" Anna whispered as she walked slowly toward him.

He suddenly remembered why he was there and began to relay his message. "I came to warn you," he whispered, his voice holding an urgent tone.

Anna's brow wrinkled in confusion. "Warn me? Of what?" she asked.

William thought he detected a slight bit of fear, but maybe he was only imagining it. "I'm not exactly sure," he admitted.

Anna's face showed even more confusion.

"My father has a wicked plan he's arranging, and I'm afraid it has something to do with you. You must get out of here!"

Anna's level response sounded through the darkness of the night and into the very core of his being. "If your father has a plan, then I'm afraid there is no chance of escape."

"But-but-" William stuttered, "you could be killed!" He had not wanted to be so blunt, but she left him no choice.

Anna's strong voice brought him nothing but confusion. "And I'm not afraid of dying," she told him clearly. "There once was a Man who left His home above in the form of a baby, so that He could one day meet a cruel, painful and shameful death. He took *my* sins and the punishment I deserved so I could be free from sin and live one day in *His* palace, and *His* Kingdom forever, for eternity! My father and mother have already gone home to that wonderful place, and I'm ready to join them the moment my Savior sees fit to take me there." Anna's voice was filled with conviction and her words confused William more than he could ever say.

"But, I thought He only died for *my* sins," William spoke, his heart beating fast.

Anna looked at him in surprise as she answered his question. "He died for *all* our sins. Has no one ever told you?"

William shook his head slowly. "I think that was what my mother was trying to tell me, on the night of her death." He told Anna of his mother's last words to him, of a Man who had died so that he might live. "But all these years I have felt awful because He died and I never got the chance to thank Him. Don't you feel the same way?" William questioned.

Anna's voice was filled with tears. "But He's not dead," she told him with a smile. "He's alive! And I *have* thanked Him, over and over and over again!"

William looked shocked, filled with disbelief.

"It's all in this," Anna held up her Bible, raising her voice just a bit. "From the creation of the world to the resurrection of Christ, it's all in here."

William held his hands out for the book, and Anna gladly gave it to him. His voice trembled with emotion. "This is the Bible?" he said.

Anna nodded, her eyes filling with sympathy. *Probably because of my ignorance*, William guessed.

William's eyes filled with tears as he flipped through the Book. "I'm not ready to die—" William's voice broke. "I'm not good enough."

Anna took a deep breath, praying for the right words. "None of us are good enough, Your Majesty," she said, her own eyes now filling with tears. "That's where God and His mercy come into place. That's why He sent His precious Son to die an awful death for us. His name is Jesus, the Name above all names. The Bible says in Philippians, that, at the end of time, at the name of Jesus, every knee shall bow: of those in Heaven, of those on earth and of those under the earth.

"*Every* knee, Your Majesty," Anna went on, "including King Raymond's. If only we repent of our sins and believe that He is the one and only way to salvation, and if we believe He died for us and rose again so that we might be saved, *that* is how we can have eternal life."

William's hands trembled as he handed the Bible back to Anna, but Anna refused to take it. "Read John 14:6 tonight, Your Honor," she requested softly.

He bid Anna a mumbled goodnight and slowly left the palace kitchen. He walked to his room as if in a daze. His whole mind cried out in protest of all he had just learned, as if refusing to believe, refusing to grasp everything.

Oh, but if only he would.

Anna returned back to her mat in the corner of the kitchen and knelt down upon the floor.

She closed her eyes and began to pray fervently for William's salvation. "Lord Jesus," she began. "You know William's heart so much better than I. Take out his heart of stone and put in its place a heart of flesh. Break his spirit of pride and replace it with a spirit of humbleness. Help him to know and understand that You are the God of the universe, in whom all things have found their being. Save him tonight, Lord Jesus, if it be Your will...."

William flipped through the pages of the Bible until he found the passage Anna had requested him to read.

"Jesus saith unto him, I am the way, the truth, and the life: no man cometh unto the Father, but by me."

Tears coursed down William's cheeks as he knelt beside his bed.

"Lord Jesus," he prayed. "I'm not a good person. I don't deserve to go to that place, where there is no more sorrow and no more pain. But I ask You now, I beg You, have mercy upon me and save my soul from hell!" A heavy burden was lifted from William's shoulders. Sobs shook his body as he continued to pray. "And thank You, Lord Jesus, for taking the punishment I deserved and dying for me. I should have died in Your place, but You took my sins upon Yourself. Thank you, Lord Jesus! Thank you!

Sixteen

Layla was worried as she began to set the table for dinner. Her daughter Amira was spending too much time with that Christian boy. She had let them play their games and she had not interfered. She had felt some pity for the fact that Caleb was an orphan, but she had let them go too far.

Amira was acting differently now, a difference Layla had not taken kindly to. Amira had even been so bold as to question the ways of Allah on a few occasions.

Layla sighed heavily as she stirred a pot of boiling stew.

She would talk to her husband tonight after the children had been put to bed. "Yes," she told herself. "He'll know what to do."

Stephen briskly walked up the steps of the dry goods store.

"Mornin', Mandy," he said with a slight smile as he stepped inside.

"Good morning, Stevie!" she replied happily, her smile lighting up her round face.

Stephen cringed inwardly at the pet name she had given him. He had endured it as a child, but now, as an almost grown man, he was thoroughly ready for a change of name.

He made his purchases quickly and tried not to tarry long.

On his way out the door, a middle-aged lady passed him. She ignored him completely and seemed to be in a great hurry. He remembered that she was the lady who owned the quilt shop down the road. "The town gossiper," everyone called her.

If they needed any information, they just went and asked Sarah. Between Sarah and Mandy, it was a wonder that there were still secrets in this world.

As he mounted his horse and turned toward home, he suddenly remembered that he had forgotten the sole purpose of his coming here. He quickly dismounted and headed back to the store for the forgotten item. The *Open* sign had been flipped to *Closed.*

That's interesting, he thought. He couldn't help but wonder what had caused the sudden change.

He tried the door and found it unlocked. Stepping inside, he left the door slightly ajar. Just as he was about to call out for assistance, he heard voices in the back of the store.

"You won't ever believe what I just heard!" Sarah exclaimed. She paused for dramatic effect.

"Well," Mandy said, exasperated. "Don't keep me in suspense!"

Stephen sighed. Couldn't they find something better to talk about?

But the next sentence made his heart quake.

"They say the king has a plan to put that scullery maid to death, because of her faith!" she burst out excitedly.

"That's awful! He can't do that!" Mandy exclaimed in shocked tones.

"Oh, but he's the king. He can do anything he wants," Sarah argued.

"Why was the king so eager for Anna to work for him?"

"Some say the king knew of her ties to Jane Willowbee."

"But why would that be reason enough to maliciously trap her into working for him?" Mandy's tone was filled with disbelief.

Sarah's eyes took on a slightly haunted look. "People have their own opinions about that one, but I believe he's trying to get even with the Lord for taking his wife's life."

Mandy gasped and her hands trembled slightly as her straightforward statement rang out. "And he thinks he can do that by taking the lives of the Lord's children."

Stephen's heart beat rapidly as he turned to leave. He couldn't listen to any more of this. He couldn't believe what he had just heard. Was Anna really in danger? Was she really going to be persecuted for her faith?

His hands trembled violently as he mounted his horse and rode for the castle.

He had to warn her, before it was too late.

Lilly hummed quietly as she washed a pile of clothes in the flowing river.

She had to admit she didn't used to like washing clothes.

But now that she was saved, she tried to look at things in a different light. She could be happy that she could wash the clothes in the river instead of having to haul buckets of snow and melt it in the kitchen, like they had to do in the winter.

She smiled inwardly as she thought of how happy Anna had been to hear of her salvation. She shouldn't have kept it inside of her for so long, but she was afraid of what Anna would say.

Her happiness was quickly replaced by worry as she thought of Prince William's startling visit last night. She couldn't help but fret over Anna's safety. What would she do if something happened to her?

Then she remembered that Anna must be wondering why she had never showed up last night.

"She might be worryin', too," Lilly said aloud.

She wrung out the last article of clothing and began to haul the heavy load to the clothesline. She usually had help with this part, but no one had shown up, so she began the daunting task alone.

She then remembered Anna had said it was a sin to worry and be anxious. *Where was that passage?* Lilly tried to remember. By the light of a candle, she had memorized the passage Anna had written down for her.

"Be careful for nothing; but in everything by prayer and supplication with thanksgiving let your

*requests be made known unto God. And the peace
of God, which passeth all understanding, shall keep
your hearts and minds through Christ Jesus."*

Was it Ruth? she asked herself. *No, that doesn't
sound right. Philippians sounds familiar,* she mused.

But her thoughts were interrupted by her mother
who had called to her to "please hurry up and come
inside."

She set about her task with renewed vigor, but
Anna's safety was never far from her mind.

*The waves of the sea violently rocked the ship to
and fro, threatening to break it to pieces. Men cried
out to their gods as they hastened to throw their
goods overboard, attempting to lighten the ship's
load. Down in the lowest part of the ship, a man lay
sleeping, the sudden storm not bothering him in the
least.*

*But the captain, perceiving that every man
aboard was not on deck, found the sleeping man and
cried out to him, saying: "What do you mean by this,
sleeper? Wake up and pray to your God. Perhaps
your God will consider us, so that we might not
perish!"*

Jonah obeyed and quickly went to the deck. He knew only too well what had caused all this.

To the right of him, men were casting lots to see who the cause of all this trouble was.

The lot fell on Jonah.

Suddenly, men surrounded him, asking him question after question.

"Who has caused all this calamity to befall us?"

"What is your occupation?"

"Where do you come from?"

"What is your country?"

"And of what people are you?"

Jonah answered them evenly, raising his voice above the storm. "I am a Hebrew, and I fear the Lord, the God of heaven, who made the sea and the dry land."

Then the men grew terribly afraid.

"Why have you done this?" For he had told the men that he had fled from the presence of the Lord. Then they asked him, "What shall we do to you so that the sea may be calm for us?"—for the sea was growing more violent by the minute.

So Jonah told them, "Pick me up and throw me into the sea, then the sea will become calm for you. For I know that all this is because of me."

Despite what he had just told them, the men rowed toward land with all their might, but it was impossible; the sea continued to grow more and more violent.

So they cried out to the Lord and said, "We pray, O Lord, please do not let us perish for this man's life, and do not charge us with innocent blood; for You, O Lord, have done as it pleased you."

So they picked up Jonah and threw him into the sea, and the sea at once grew calm.

Agnes walked away from her window with a heavy sigh.

What an awful thing to happen to Jonah!

Surely he couldn't have lived through all that, but what a miracle that the sea was calm the moment they threw him in.

She had read the beginning of the story of Jonah yesterday evening and hadn't been able to stop thinking about it since.

Picking up a small bell, she rang for her maid, who answered almost immediately.

"What can I do for ya, ma'am?" she asked Agnes.

"I would like some tea brought to my room, please," she asked her kindly.

As the maid turned to leave, Agnes called out again.

"Oh, and Margaret, please look for that new scullery maid. I need to consult with her on a matter."

The maid's eyebrows rose slightly, but she was taught not to question orders, so she merely nodded and went to do as she was told.

She was gone for only a short while, then returned bearing a golden tray tastefully arranged with a silver teapot which contained the choicest tea. Also on the tray were several delicacies: scones, raspberry tarts and tiny meat pies. They were surrounded by the prettiest blue cornflowers Agnes had ever seen.

"Oh, Margaret, these are beautiful! Did you pick them?"

When Margaret replied she did, Agnes offered her a beautiful smile and thanked her again.

Margaret didn't seem to know what to do with so much praise, so she blushed and curtsied and walked out the door almost all at once.

Agnes placed the pretty cornflowers on a table by the chair she occupied and set to work on her tea.

I might go and take the carriage around the park soon, she thought.

It had been awhile since she had taken her once daily trek through the city's popular attraction.

But Agnes couldn't stop thinking about what happened to Jonah next...

Jonah hit the waters below and plunged beneath the cold waves.

The raging sea at once grew calm. He kicked, trying to resurface, but to no avail. He tried to breathe, but was only greeted by a mouthful of salty water.

Now, the Lord had prepared a fish who was swimming straight toward Jonah.

Without any warning, the fish opened his large, daunting mouth and swallowed Jonah.

"I do think that would be more terrifying than drowning." Agnes reflected.

At that moment a maid knocked on her door and came to retrieve her tray. Agnes called out just as Margaret began to leave. "Oh, Margaret, did you ever find Anna?" She hadn't meant to let the name slip out, but it was too late now.

Margaret shook her head. "I's couldn't find her anywheres, ma'am," she said, in an apologetic tone.

"That's all right," Agnes sighed. "Thank you for looking."

The maid exited the room and Agnes grabbed her Bible from under her bed.

Strange, she thought to herself. *Anna never came here last night and Margaret couldn't find her now. I'm sure she's just busy here and there. I shouldn't borrow trouble*, she concluded.

She decided to read the rest of the story of Jonah, at least his prayer in the belly of the giant fish...

From inside the fish, Jonah prayed to the LORD his God. He said:

"In trouble, deep trouble, I prayed to God.
He answered me.
From the belly of the grave I cried, 'Help!'
You heard my cry.
You threw me into ocean's depths,
into a watery grave,
With ocean waves, ocean breakers
crashing over me.
I said, 'I've been thrown away,
thrown out, out of Your sight.
I'll never again lay eyes

on Your Holy Temple.'
Ocean gripped me by the throat.
The ancient Abyss grabbed me and held tight.
My head was all tangled in seaweed
at the bottom of the sea where the mountains take
root.
I was as far down as a body can go,
and the gates were slamming shut behind me
forever—
Yet You pulled me up from that grave alive,
O God, my God!
When my life was slipping away,
I remembered God,
And my prayer got through to You,
made it all the way to Your Holy Temple.
Those who worship hollow gods, god-frauds,
walk away from their only true love.
But I'm worshiping You, God,
calling out in thanksgiving!
And I'll do what I promised I'd do!
Salvation belongs to God!'
Salvation comes from the LORD."

Agnes closed her Bible with a smile.

She would save the rest for after she came back from her ride.

Surely, God wouldn't let Jonah die. After hearing a prayer like that, she felt quite sorry for the poor man.

But if God did not choose to save Jonah, then He must have had a sufficient reason, Agnes was sure.

One thing was for certain, Jonah got it right when he said, *'salvation comes from the Lord.'*

Seventeen

William went about his duties that day with a joyful heart. He had at long last found the Man who'd taken his punishment, only to discover that the Man wasn't just a man, but also the Creator, the Maker of the universe and the Creator of his being.

His heart sang within him as he paced his room, but he still had many questions that needed answers. The main one being, *why had he never been told about this Man?*

However, worry for Anna's safety was never far from him. He had to find a way to keep her safe. Suddenly, he thought of something.

"Grandmother!" he exclaimed, snapping his fingers and stopping mid-stride. "She'll know what to do."

He ran up the palace stairs two steps at a time. When he reached her door, he knocked twice before entering. But she wasn't there.

William's brow furrowed in confusion. She usually didn't leave her room this time in the afternoon. Come to think of it, she'd actually kept to her room quite often the past few months.

He walked over to her window and brushed the curtain aside. A carriage was departing, the royal carriage at that.

It wouldn't be his Father, he mused. He'd just seen him going into the library. Maybe she was feeling better, and decided to take a trip into town.

He decided to discreetly look for Anna and see if she had carried out her plan to visit Grandmother last night. Maybe that had something to do with her absence.

But after looking for over half an hour, he was convinced Anna had gone out as well.

He inquired of the servants, but they were positive she had not gone into town. William's heart sank as he continued his fruitless search. He was only too happy when he heard the rumble of the carriage on the cobblestone drive.

He ran out to greet Agnes, with only one thought in mind.

"Grandmother!" William called out.

"William?" Agnes asked, a look of slight confusion etching her features. William offered his hand to assist her down from the carriage.

"I need to speak with you," he said hastily.

Agnes suggested they speak in her room.

As they walked into her bedroom, William glanced outside her door, making certain that no one was within earshot. "I can't find Anna anywhere!" he burst out, his voice filling with urgency.

Agnes placed her hat upon the dresser and took off her gloves, placing them beside her hat. "What makes you think I know of that scullery maid's whereabouts?" she asked slyly.

She sat down upon her window seat and folded her hands neatly upon her lap.

William sat at a low stool by her feet. "Please don't play games, Grandmother," he asked her kindly. "I know you have befriended Anna. She is missing and I need your help."

Agnes answered him evenly. "And what is she to you, my boy?"

William glanced briefly at her face. "A friend, Grandmother. A friend who told me about the One who saved my soul from hell and took the punishment I deserve upon Himself so I could live someday within His home for eternity!"

Agnes gasped. "You don't mean?" she began, daring to hope her assumption was true.

"Yes, Grandmother," he said. "Last night I gave my life to Christ."

Agnes's eyes filled with tears as she held her grandson's face between her aged hands. "I have been praying for you, my boy. Ever since the Lord saved me and showed me the right way."

William stood up and began to pace the room. "I can't find Anna anywhere, and I have started to grow anxious."

Agnes's face paled. "She never came here last night," she whispered in fear.

"You're telling me, she never showed up at all?" William asked, pacing the floor a few more times before going to sit on the edge of her bed. As he looked at her, his face grew pale as well.

Agnes shook her head slowly. "You don't think...?" she began.

William shook his head. "I refuse to think anything before I get a solid lead!" He groaned, putting his face in his hands. "If anything happened to her, it would be my fault."

A confused look passed over Agnes's face. "What do you mean, William? Why would it be *your* fault?"

"I brought her here and procured this position for her." He lifted his head from his hands and looked at his grandmother, a haunted look in his eyes. He then told her from the beginning all that had happened: how they had found Anna passed out from dehydration and malnourishment; how he helped to secure a room for her; and finally, how he had offered her a job. He also told her how he had tried to stop her from signing the paper. "Don't you see?" he finished. "It would be my fault if something happened!"

Agnes's eyes were filled with tears. "No, William," she said quietly. "I don't see."

William looked at her in surprise as she continued. "All I see, is a man who has put his own life aside while practically saving another's. All I see, is my grandson who has humbled himself enough to accept the gift of salvation. And what I see is a picture of Christ, willing to sacrifice everything to save the life of another." Agnes looked William steadily in the eye. "You sound like the old William—the William who used to lean on his own understanding, and only trust his own powers. But, my dear boy, you have Christ's understanding to lean on now, as well as *His* powers to guide you every step of the way. Whatever happens to Anna, you cannot change. Whatever happens is God's will, and that, my boy, cannot be stopped."

William's eyes filled with tears as he went to embrace his grandmother. Until this moment, he had not truly realized how precious she was to him.

"Come, my boy, and listen to the Words which have brought me much comfort and joy. And then we will go together to look for Anna."

She flipped through her Bible and read the passages she had bookmarked while William sat on the floor by her feet and listened closely to the words of the Lord.

"Come unto me, all ye that labor and are heavy laden, and I will give you rest. Take my yoke upon you, and learn of me; for I am meek and lowly in heart: and ye shall find rest unto your souls. For my yoke is easy, and my burden is light."

"Be anxious for nothing, but in everything by prayer and supplication, with thanksgiving, let your requests be made known to God; and the peace of God, which surpasses all understanding, will guard your hearts and minds through Christ Jesus."

"Thou wilt shew me the path of life: in thy presence is fullness of joy; at thy right hand there are pleasures for evermore."

Anna woke with a feeling that something was terribly amiss.

Where was she? Surely not in the kitchen. The room was pitch dark and only an occasional drip of water could be heard.

Beneath her was not the mat she had grown accustomed to, but cold, hard stone.

She sat up, pulling her shawl closer around her shoulders, shivering from the draft. Or was it from fright? She wasn't sure.

Her heart beat wildly within her as she realized that she was nowhere that she had been before. It was too dark to see, but something inside of Anna told her that she was in unfamiliar territory.

Sitting up slowly, she tightly held her head and moaned softly.

She tried to think back to what happened, but everything was hazy. She couldn't remember, and her head hurt terribly.

Slowly, bit by bit, it all began to come back.

She had planned on going to visit Grandmother with Lilly, but Lilly never arrived. William had come to warn her. They talked about Christ and the story of redemption. She had knelt to pray for him.

But what had happened after that?

She tried hard to remember. She had started up the stairs to Grandmother's room when someone grabbed her from behind.

She had tried to scream, but no sound had come.

She remembered kicking and trying to escape from her captor's grasp.

But then everything had gone black.

"Did you get her?" the king asked greedily.

Ahmad looked down at his shoes and nodded.

"Well, where is she?" Raymond asked.

"In the dungeon, sir," Ahmad answered, looking up at him.

The king knew, of course, where Anna had been taken, but he wanted to hear it from Ahmad himself.

From somewhere within his soul, Ahmad found the courage to go on. "I'm finished working for you, sir," he dared to utter the words. "I am ready to lead an honorable life, one I can be proud—"

The king cut him off. "If you value your worthless little life, then I would suggest you take back those words!" His hate-filled eyes were glued on Ahmad's face. "If you do not, it will be the last mistake you will ever make!"

The king did not flinch as he awaited Ahmad's answer.

Ahmad slowly lifted his face to the king's and looked him in the eye, but he couldn't bring himself to say the words he had rehearsed over and over again. He nodded his head slowly, admitting defeat.

Anna stood up and felt her way along the cold walls.

"I'm in a dungeon," she said, her voice hoarse and sounding nothing like her own.

Anna jumped in fright as her words echoed against the stone walls and throughout the room, only confirming the fact that she was a captive. She breathed deeply, trying to calm her panicked mind.

A deep sigh escaped her lips as she sat back down in the corner of the small room. A tear slid down her cheek and she brushed it angrily away. "Look at yourself!" she scolded, as one tear followed another.

"*You*, who have talked and talked about being ready to die for Christ, are crying just because you have finally come to the place where you knew you would be someday."

Please, Lord, she prayed silently, *give me the strength to get through this, even if it comes to giving my life for You. Give me peace, Lord Jesus. Help me to be like Paul and Silas who sang praises in Your name even though they were suffering.*

Anna drifted off to sleep thinking of the verse she had memorized only weeks before:

"Therefore we are always confident, knowing that, whilst we are at home in the body, we are absent from the Lord. For we walk by faith, not by sight. We are confident, I say, and willing rather to be absent from the body, and to be present with the Lord."

Eighteen

William was breathing heavily from running up and down the palace stairs. He and Grandmother had searched and searched, but Anna was nowhere to be found. He brought Grandmother a report every so often, at her request. After the first hour of fruitless searching, he had convinced her to rest.

But he was discouraged to once again relay that he had found nothing, no sign of where Anna had gone. Or where she had been taken to. William shuddered at the thought.

He had to find out what happened, and he had to find out quickly.

As he entered Grandmother's room, he told her of his plan. "I'm going underground," he said, refusing to refer to it as the *dungeon*.

He shrugged into a light coat he had brought with him.

"Are you sure?" Agnes asked, placing a gentle hand on his arm.

William turned and looked his beloved grandmother in the eye. "Yes," he replied, his voice steady, "I'm sure."

He gently embraced Agnes and entreated her to pray for him, to which she replied that he didn't even need to ask. She wouldn't stop praying until she heard from him again.

William walked softly down the stairs, keeping a watchful eye out for his father.

He walked through the Great Hall, and the Ballroom, both empty with an eeriness about them. He exited the rooms, turning his direction toward a narrow tunnel. He quickened his pace and was soon near the door leading to the prison.

He took a deep breath and prayed for the first time that he *wouldn't* find Anna. At least not down here.

Exhaling slowly, he opened the door and began the descent down the long flight of stairs.

The stairs were lit by brightly burning torches, tossing ghostly shadows against the walls. William noticed that the further he went, the colder it became.

And the further he went, the more his prayers intensified. *Please, dear Lord,* he prayed silently, *don't let me find her down here…. Please!*

Agnes knelt before her bedside, folding her hands in prayer.

"Dear Lord and Savior Jesus Christ," she began, her voice quivering with emotion. "Please protect Anna wherever she may be. Help her not to grow discouraged, but please put a blanket of peace around her now. Help her not to be afraid. Lord, I pray she might not be in terrible trouble, though I feel inside of me that it might be so.

"Please bring her peace, and even joy, in the situation she is in. Help her to know You will never leave her nor forsake her. Help her to know she is loved by You and many others. Help protect my grandson as he tries to find her. Help him to trust in You and call out to You in his distress. Help us, Lord, and protect us from the evil ways of my son. Break my son's heart of stone and fill it with Your love...."

Anna sat up again, feeling refreshed after her nap.

Her present state dawned upon her again, and she began to grow discouraged.

But as quickly as it came, the distress was replaced by a feeling she couldn't quite put into words, although she was very aware of its presence. It settled around her as if it were a blanket, filling her with hope, joy and peace.

She was reminded that this earth was not her home, but she was only camping here, so to speak, until the Lord saw fit to take her to her true home.

Standing up, she let her eyes slowly adjust to the soft light now burning a few feet away.

She could better see her surroundings, and for that, she was grateful. Her mind tried to grasp one of the many Bible verses she had committed to memory, but her brain didn't seem to work properly. She stood in front of the iron bars, the only thing keeping her captive, and began to sing.

She sang softly, almost whispering, but she gradually grew louder and louder until her beautiful voice floated gently down the halls of the dark dungeon, bouncing off the walls and seeming to chase all the darkness away.

Her fear subsided for the present as she continued to sing:

Rock of Ages, cleft for me,
let me hide myself in thee;

let the water and the blood,
from thy wounded side which flowed,
be of sin the double cure;
save from wrath and make me pure.

Not the labors of my hands
can fulfill thy law's demands;
could my zeal no respite know,
could my tears forever flow,
all for sin could not atone;
thou must save, and thou alone.

Nothing in my hand I bring,
simply to the cross I cling;
naked, come to thee for dress;
helpless, look to thee for grace;
foul, I to the fountain fly;
wash me, Savior, or I die.

While I draw this fleeting breath,
when mine eyes shall close in death,
when I soar to worlds unknown,
see thee on thy judgment throne,
Rock of Ages, cleft for me,
let me hide myself in thee.

Layla brushed her fingers through her silky black hair, waiting patiently for her husband to come to bed. He was taking his time in telling his little daughters goodnight. She was grateful to have such a loving and caring husband. Allah had been kind to her indeed.

At long last, Sadan came into his room. Layla decided not to tarry in telling him of her thoughts. "I need to speak with you on a matter," she began.

"Hmm?" was his only response.

Layla let his disinterest pass and pressed on. "Amira has been spending too much time with Caleb, in my opinion. She has begun to question the ways of Allah!" Her eyes were wide as she broke the news to her husband.

But Sadan didn't seem to be surprised. "All children will question our ways and beliefs, at one time or another. They have before and always will, most likely. Don't see any reason to get all riled up about it."

He seemed to be finished; he crawled under the covers and blew out the light, leaving Layla in the dark.

But she wasn't so easily convinced.

She still thought something strange was going on and she was determined to put a stop to Caleb's visits.

With a sigh, she scooted under the covers and closed her eyes.

"Who goes there?" Stephen's voice echoed through the darkness of the palace prison.

William took a deep breath and steadied himself before answering. "It is I, Prince William," he spoke softly, not knowing why he felt the need to whisper; Stephen definitely hadn't.

William heard footsteps and soon, Stephen's face came into view, one hand tightly holding the sword hanging by his side. His face showed both surprise and relief. "What brings you down here, Your Highness?" Stephen asked, his voice filled with curiosity.

William took a deep breath. "You don't happen to have within your possession a certain scullery maid, do you?"

When Stephen didn't answer, William began to describe her. "She's about yea tall," William said, measuring with his hand. "Brown hair and brown eyes—"

"I know what she looks like, Your Highness," Stephen said curtly.

"She's down here?" William's voice returned to a whisper.

Stephen shook his head. "I didn't say that, I only said that I knew what she looked like."

William was quickly growing impatient. "Is she down here or not, Stephen?" he asked, his words coming out rougher than he meant.

He noticed a slight scowl cover Stephen's face.

Stephen hesitated as long as he dared before answering. "Yes, she's here," he admitted. His tone was dead and his words couldn't have made William feel any sicker.

William made a movement as if to walk past him, but Stephen stuck out his arm and stepped to the side, blocking his way.

William's eyebrows shot up in surprise. "What do you mean by detaining me?" His tone was filled with shock.

"It is what your father would want and you know it," Stephen shot back.

"What my father wants is not usually the best," William told him wisely. "And I think you of all people can attest to that." When Stephen didn't answer, William continued. "You can use this as a chance to redeem yourself, Stephen."

Stephen knew only too well what he meant. "What if I don't want to be redeemed?"

William didn't hesitate to answer his challenge. "What we want and what we need are two completely different things." He tried to sidestep him, but he was once again blocked by Stephen's body.

"What if I don't *need* to be redeemed?" Stephen challenged.

William was quick in offering his reply. "Everyone needs to be redeemed. We need redemption through Jesus Christ to have salvation. You can still have a second chance, Stephen," William told him, his tone filling with compassion. "You don't have to keep living the life you're living! You're going to kill yourself with the guilt resting upon your shoulders. You don't need to be the one who carries that burden any longer. You still have time to be forgiven for the things you have done, but you need to do it before it's too late."

Stephens face grew hard as stone. "Have you ever killed someone you loved, because of a sin you committed?" His voice was filled with anger, his jaw clamped tight.

William was thoughtful as he answered his inquiry. "Yes," he replied. "I have." William then went on to explain. "Because of my own sins, I put the dearest Person who ever roamed the face of this

earth upon a tree to die in humiliation and agony."
William's voice wavered with emotion. "But
because He died, I am now free, and He has forgiven
me for the sins that put Him to death. And you can
have that freedom and forgiveness, too, Stephen, if
only you ask!"

William's words had the desired effect, for
Stephen's face was slowly losing its hardened look;
slowly, a new look passed over Stephen's face, a look
of distress and utter sadness. His chin quivered with
emotion and sobs shook his body as he turned away.

William went on to tell Stephen how to accept
the gift of salvation that had been granted to him by
the sacrifice Christ had made on his behalf.

Stephen gladly accepted it and gave his life and
soul to Christ.

For how long they stood there talking, William
didn't know.

Stephen wiped the tears off his cheeks and
repeatedly thanked William. "I don't know what I
would have done if you hadn't come along," Stephen
told him. "I don't want a repeat of what happened a
few months ago," he said with conviction.

William then asked Stephen if he could show him
the way to Anna.

On their way, Stephen voiced his opinion on the
matter at hand. "You cannot just take her out and
find some way of escape," he started. "The king has
spies surrounding the castle. It would be unwise to

try and take such a risk." An apologetic look swept over his features. "I-I didn't mean *you* would be unwise, Your Highness," he stuttered, his face turning crimson red.

William pretended not to notice. "I would like for you to be open and frank with me, Stephen," he replied. "And I have a feeling we are going to need to work together to get her out of here. We can't have hurt feelings getting in the way."

Anna stood up as she heard voices coming her way.

Walking to the front of her cell, she took a deep breath and braced herself for what was to come. Relief filled her when she saw William rounding the corner, walking briskly toward her.

But then it hit her. Had William betrayed her after she had been so open with him? Had he been the one who caused all this? She refused to believe anything her mind was telling her. Not until she heard what he had to say.

William looked up just as Anna came forward. Anna placed her hands upon the cold bars, silently waiting for William to speak.

But as William stopped in front of the bars, he was at a loss for what to say. He couldn't very well tell her everything was going to be alright, because he didn't know if that was the truth. He couldn't just apologize and then walk away.

Just as he was about to say something, Stephen broke the silence. "You won't ever believe what just happened!" he told Anna, his eyes bright with excitement. "William and I had a great talk, one I wished we'd had a long time ago, and I gave my life to Christ!"

Although he had never even spoken to Anna before, it seemed the right thing to say. He also hoped it would help to break the awkward silence. But he mentally cringed at how immature the words sounded.

William looked horrified.

"Stephen!" he hissed through his teeth, "Her life is in jeopardy; the last thing she wants to hear is *that!*"

Anna didn't know at first if Stephen was mocking her or telling the truth, but upon William's outburst she decided to believe the latter.

"On the contrary," she said, as a gentle smile lit her face. "There is nothing that would bring me more joy right now than to hear that another soul in this palace has become a follower of Christ." Both young men looked at her in surprise. Anna continued, "Does that mean you gave your life to

Christ as well?" she questioned William, daring to hope her prayers had been answered.

William nodded. "Thanks to you I am no longer the man I used to be, and many of the questions that have plagued me for half of my life have now been answered."

Anna smiled joyously. "Thanks be to God!" she murmured, her voice filled with happiness despite her present condition.

"I am going to try my best in finding you a way out of here," William assured her.

Anna thanked him quietly, but she knew deep down inside that it would be almost impossible.

Stephen was quiet during the whole exchange as he tried his best to think of a plan to get Anna out without being caught. If they were caught, they could be imprisoned themselves, or even worse. Stephen shuddered. Being caught wouldn't solve any of their problems.

William slipped off his coat and handed it through the bars of Anna's cell. It was the least he could do.

Anna accepted the coat gratefully. She slipped it over her slender shoulders, not caring that it almost swallowed her small frame. She was at once thankful for the warmth it brought.

With a parting promise that they would return as soon as possible, they left Anna to the confines of her dwelling.

But Anna didn't seem to mind her present state.

She was still marveling and rejoicing at the fact that, bit by bit, God was showing His mercy on this dark and depressing kingdom.

And, bit by bit, lights were being added to the palace.

A small smile lit Anna's face as she remembered her conversation with Agnes. She hoped with all her might that soon, all darkness would be chased away.

Nineteen

The king paced his library, deep in thought. He couldn't just sentence her to death, he told himself.

Not without a fair trial, he smiled within himself.

But if she was anything like her aunt, she wouldn't be frightened by anything. Not anything that would be harmful to *her* body.

Then he thought of a plan. "Yes," he said aloud. "Yes, that's what I'll do."

A wicked smile slowly spread across his face.

He laughed happily. He was very clever, yes, very clever indeed!

Agnes must have fallen asleep praying; when she awoke, she was still kneeling. She stood up slowly, her knees aching in protest.

She walked over to her chair by the window, her favorite chair lined with royal blue velvet. It had been her daughter-in-law's favorite color.

Agnes waited somewhat impatiently for William to return. She was beginning to grow anxious again until she finally heard his steps outside her door. She tried to stand up, but her legs wouldn't work.

William walked in and closed the door somewhat loudly behind him. He had the most interesting look on his face, Agnes thought. A strange look of both utter joy and utter sadness.

She held her breath. "Well? What did you find out?"

"She's down there," he replied, his voice tense.

Agnes gasped and her face turned pale. "We must get her out of there!"

William tried to calm her. "We need to pray. There isn't anything else we can do right now."

Tears filled Agnes's eyes. "But we can't just sit here and watch her die!" she said, almost harshly.

"I don't intend to," William retorted, biting his tongue to keep from saying more. "But Father has guards and spies placed everywhere in this castle. It would be unwise to try to take action now without a plan," he said, using Stephen's words.

Agnes's face gained back some of its color and she submitted to what William was saying.

She had been praying, and she would continue to pray.

She then learned why William had also looked happy when he first stepped into the room. He told her of Stephen's confession and how he had been saved.

Agnes was as joyful as she could be, despite the present circumstances. After a moment of silence, she asked William to pray with her. They knelt beside her bed, William taking his grandmother's wrinkled hand in his strong, youthful one.

For how long they were down there, they didn't know. They lost track of all time, only knowing one thing: they needed a miracle.

All they could do was ask.

Caleb was more excited than he could say.

His sisters were coming to stay a few days! Mr. and Mrs. Autry were going to visit their daughter's family a few hours away.

Two exciting things in one week. His heart was overfilled with joy.

He waited as patiently as a ten-year-old boy could wait, and at long last, the familiar Autry family wagon pulled up to their house.

He ran out the front door as fast as his legs could carry him.

Margret and Julianna jumped down from the wagon and ran to greet their older brother. Caleb embraced his little sisters and they began sharing the exciting things they were to do the next few days.

They turned to wave goodbye as the wagon rumbled away. "Bye, Maman!" yelled four-year-old Margret, waving her little hand as fast as it would go.

Caleb noticed nine-year-old Julianna's slight scowl at Margret's *Maman*," but he decided to let it go for now.

Margret needed both a mother and a father-figure in her young life, and he personally didn't see any problem in her calling Mr. and Mrs. Autry *Maman* and *Papa.* But apparently, Julianna felt differently.

"Come inside," Caleb offered, giving an arm to each of them. "You won't ever guess from whom I received a letter!" he exclaimed happily as they strolled into the family sitting room.

"Then what's the point in guessing?" Julianna's straightforward answer rang out.

Caleb smiled as he leaned down to Margret's level. He sat her on the sofa and gave her braids a playful tug. "Can you try to guess?" he challenged her.

"Was it from Anna?" she asked, her little voice filled with hope.

"Yes!" Caleb replied, picking her up and spinning her around in a circle. Margret's carefree laughter filled the room, causing smiles all around.

Julianna was equally excited. "What did it say?" she asked Caleb, tugging gently on his sleeve.

Caleb stopped spinning. He set Margret down and she grabbed onto his leg, sitting on top of his foot.

Mrs. Banks poked her head around the corner, a smile lighting up her pretty face. "Try to keep it down, you three," she told them. "Isaiah's trying to sleep."

"Yes, ma'am," they chorused.

"I waited for both of you," Caleb answered. He was slightly hurt that she had expected him to have already read the letter.

Julianna's heart swelled with love for her brother. She knew waiting didn't come very easily to him.

Caleb walked awkwardly over to the sofa, Margret still clinging onto his leg. He sat down and picked Margret up, setting her gently upon his knee. Carefully, he pulled the letter out of his pocket.

He ripped it open and slid out the folded sheet of paper.

With an excited voice, he began to read aloud: *"Dear Caleb, Margret, Juliana, and Isaiah—"*

"Isaiah's not here!" Margret interrupted unhappily.

"Well, you'll just have to tell him about it when he wakes up from his nap," Caleb answered.

"He would enjoy hearing it from you better, anyhow," Caleb told her kindly. He took a deep breath and went back to reading: *"How I have missed you all and each of your sweet personalities! I hope you have not missed me too dreadfully. I pray for each of you every day and hope you have not been too much trouble for the kind families who have opened their homes to you. I can hardly grasp the fact that we have been parted for almost three months now! You will find it hard to believe what the Lord has been seeing me through lately. Guess what? I have been hired to work for the king! It is a job which requires a good bit of work, and I am thankful our Mother and Father taught us that hard work wouldn't kill us!*

You all don't remember Aunt Jane, but the reason I am working for the king is because she died shortly before I docked here in Carpathia. The boat ride here was quite pleasant, though I did get seasick twice. It took a while before I got my 'sea legs,' as the ship's captain called them.

I would appreciate your prayers for me concerning a matter I wouldn't want to bother your little minds over, so I shall suffice it to say, just pray that I would be strengthened and encouraged, both mentally and physically, and that I would be willing to give everything up for Christ. I love each of you very dearly and you are in my prayers every day. Give Isaiah a kiss for me!

May our Lord and Savior, Jesus Christ, bless each of you.

Your loving sister and friend—Anna."

The threesome was quiet for a while as they soaked in every word Anna had written.

Then, Caleb suggested they go into town for a treat. He had been saving the coins he had earned from getting groceries for their neighbor and chopping wood for the church's fire to use when winter comes.

They were all in agreement on the matter and went to ask permission; it was granted, and they set off for the dry goods store, eagerly awaiting the rare treat.

Agnes wiped away the tears that had found their way down her wrinkled cheeks.

William had left her room a few hours ago, but Agnes had continued praying. She felt like God was telling her to go and talk with her son. She didn't want to; if she caught him at a bad time, there was no telling what he might do. She felt as if she were being told to do it. She ignored it at first, but the prompting kept growing louder and louder, stronger and stronger until she at last cried out, "I'll go, Lord! I'll go!"

She determined that if God was telling her to do something, she needn't worry about her own safety—just like God had protected Esther, He would protect *her*.

With steady steps, she found her son, reclining comfortably in a large plush chair in the corner of the spacious library. As she walked toward him, he didn't look up. *He must be very involved in his book,* Agnes thought to herself.

Then she caught sight of the title: *How to Bend Others to Your Will, with Harmless and Not So Harmless Methods.*

Agnes shivered, and it wasn't from the draft that had just blown through the library window.

A smile spread over the king's face and he glanced up from his book. But as he looked up and saw his mother, his smile was replaced by an ugly scowl. "What do you want?" he mumbled grumpily.

Agnes took a deep breath and prayed for God's guidance before answering. "I just wanted to entreat you not to do anything you might someday regret," she began. The king's scowl deepened, but he said nothing. Agnes, feeling a wave of security around her, continued. "What you have been doing and what you are planning to do is both wicked and shameful, not only to your name," she hesitated, "but also to the name of the Lord."

She waited for the expected blow to come, but the king only sat there as if turned to stone. So, feeling quite brave, Agnes continued. "This is not what Isabelle would have wanted, nor your father," she said gently. "I beg you to change your ways before the Lord begins to change them for you."

She dared to leave him with a parting scripture.

"If my people, which are called by my name, shall humble themselves, and pray, and seek my face, and turn from their wicked ways; then will I hear from heaven, and will forgive their sin, and will heal their land."

"What did the banana say to the squirrel?" Margret's childlike chatter rang out through the small store.

They had purchased a half pound of candies and sat in the corner of the store on long wooden benches. Julianna groaned at her little sister's joke. Evidently, this wasn't the first time she had heard it.

"I don't know." Caleb played along, a smile tugging at the corners of his mouth. "What did the banana say to the squirrel?"

Margret giggled. "Nothing. Bananas can't talk!"

Caleb laughed heartily at his little sister's joke, and even though Julianna had heard it many times before, she laughed along with them.

The shopkeeper couldn't help but smile as well.

Caleb searched through the bag for a strip of licorice and handed it to Margret.

He wished for one moment that he could be like little Margret, with not a care in the world.

Margret was quiet for a moment as she took a bite of her candy, her small eyes closing as she savored the flavor.

"Did you get permission to go to the fair on Saturday, Julie?" Caleb asked her, taking advantage of the moment of silence.

Julianna was happy to hear her favorite nickname again. She nodded her head quickly. "Mr. and Mrs. Autry said we could be a part of the parade! And we can even stay real late 'til they shoot the fireworks!"

Her tone was filled with excitement, which Caleb shared wholeheartedly.

They talked about the fair for a while longer while they finished the last of their candies. Soon, they stood up to leave. On their way out, the monthly newspaper caught Caleb's eye.

The heading read:

King of Carpathia Gone Mad: Holding Christians Hostage, Threatening Their Lives.

Caleb told his sisters to wait outside for him. He picked up the newspaper and asked the shopkeeper how much it cost.

"You can just have it if you really want it," he replied with a smile. "The wrong shipment of papers came in, and we received those instead of the correct ones. Don't have any need for the Carpathia news."

Caleb thanked him, folded the paper and tucked it into his back pocket. He went out to join his sisters, but the joy had gone out of his day. His mouth was dry, and he found it difficult to breathe. He prayed with everything in him that the newspaper he held had nothing to do with Anna, but somewhere deep within his soul, he felt that something was terribly amiss.

Anna stood up as the king came striding towards her. She had no idea what he had in mind. Taking a deep breath, she took a step back and braced herself.

He stepped forward, a daunting smile upon his lips. "You have one chance to renounce your faith, my dear, or you join your aunt, wherever it was she went."

Anna looked up at him and answered without wavering, "My aunt went to heaven, Your Highness, and that's exactly where I shall be going, whether you are the one to send me there or not."

Anna's straightforward answer would have caught most people off guard, but if it happened to the king, he didn't show it. "You still haven't answered my question." He fidgeted impatiently.

Anna thought what she had told him was answer enough, but apparently not. Her voice rang out evenly. "My answer, Your Majesty, is no."

The king's face never changed as he continued. "You will, by great means, regret that answer." Turning, he left her with those words.

Anna knew she would by *no* means regret her answer. It was an answer she believed in and knew to be right.

Standing there, looking after the king's retreating figure, Anna's heart grew hard against him, after what he had done to her aunt and was now planning to do to her. She knew she could not hate him, for hating was as bad as the sin he himself was about to commit. But she couldn't help despising him for all he had done. Anna sank down slowly to the cold stone floor, pulling her knees up to her chest and wrapping her arms around them. Then with a shuddering sigh, she rested her head against her knees and wept.

Twenty

The king quickly slipped under his coverlet. He was on edge; for what reason, he could not say.

His mother's visit in the library was not only strange, but also a bit frightening. He had been jumping at every sound and creak he heard thereafter. What did she mean by saying that the Lord would change his ways? It was most frightening, indeed.

He would have usually brushed aside her comments, but what she had said seemed startling. He tried his best to rest, but sleep wouldn't come.

His mother's words still rang sharply in his ear. *This is not what Isabelle would have wanted...you need to change your ways before the Lord changes them for you!*

The king sat upright, grasping his head and talking to himself.

At the sight of him, one would think he had gone quite mad.

But regardless of the king's efforts, the voices refused to leave. So, laying back down on his bed, he prepared himself for a very long night.

The next day, the king sat at the breakfast table, eating his food slowly. He was tired from his restless night and blamed his mother. When he had eaten as much as he possibly could, he stood and signaled for Ahmad to follow him.

Ahmad, who had been waiting patiently for the king to finish, was quickly at his side. After the king's threat, he had made every possible effort to be on his best behavior, going above and beyond so as not to anger him any further than he already had. He followed the king obediently to the palace library. But what Raymond had to say was short.

"I want you to find that young maid Anna has been talking to and bring her to me."

Ahmad knew exactly what King Raymond was requesting, which was exactly the reason he hesitated. The king's eyebrows shot up in a questioning stare.

Ahmad bowed quickly. "As you wish, Your Majesty." His voice was as stiff as his bow.

He turned to leave, the king's voice following him as he went. "And do it quickly!"

Ahmad nodded and went to do as he was told. He hoped the young girl wouldn't give him as much trouble as Anna had.

After a lengthy search, he found her gathering herbs in the garden. She was humming a charming tune; one he had not heard before.

He felt like a monster; he couldn't possibly cause harm to come to this child. But he knew he had no choice.

He would start out with a kind approach, and if that didn't work, he would have to take more drastic measures. Ahmad wasn't sure if he was relieved or frightened that Lilly noticed him first. Her brown eyes looked at him curiously; there wasn't even a bit of fear in them.

Ahmad approached her slowly, his voice coming out no louder than a whisper. "I know where your friend is," he told her.

Lilly's face lit up as he spoke. "Where is she?" Lilly whispered back, standing up and dusting off her apron.

"Come with me and I will show you," Ahmad offered.

Lilly usually would not have followed without feeling at least a little apprehensive, but she was desperate to know of Anna's whereabouts. She followed him without thinking, not knowing that it was all a trap.

Caleb ate his dinner quickly and excused himself from the table.

He was glad his sisters were still eating; this would give him time to find out what the newspaper was all about.

He ran up to his room and closed the door behind him.

Dropping down onto his knees, he pulled the newspaper out from under the boards of his bedframe and read the heading again, praying for the hundredth time that evening that Anna had nothing to do with it.

"Christian Jane Willowbee killed for her faith. The public mourns the terrible loss. Another Christian is being held prisoner by the king. Should we let this injustice continue?

Write to The Watchmen Newspaper Company, 137 Whitefield Lane, if you are willing to stand against this corruption!

Caleb was terrified. Aunt Jane was killed? That's why Anna was forced to work for the king. He knew Anna was the one being held prisoner, he just knew it!

Running quickly down the stairs to the kitchen, he was glad to see that Mrs. Bonnaire was alone. The table had been cleared and his sisters were nowhere in sight.

"It's true, isn't it?" Caleb asked, his voice breaking with emotion. He held up the newspaper for Mrs. Bonnaire to see.

"I had hoped that you wouldn't see that." Her tone was full of sympathy as she bent down to his level and encircled him in a gentle hug. She let him cry while offering soothing words in his ear. "Mr. Bonnaire and I are doing everything within our power to get her out of there. We've written to the newspaper company. We have even written a letter to the king. Short of going there, we have tried everything we could possibly think of, and we won't stop trying." She gave him one last hug and wiped away his tears. "We must pray for Anna, harder than we have ever prayed before."

Caleb nodded, very thankful at this moment for Mrs. Bonnaire, who had agreed to take him and Isaiah in when their father died.

As he turned to leave the kitchen, Mrs. Bonnaire called after him.

"It may not be wise to tell your sisters quite yet. It would ruin the short time you have with each other."

Caleb nodded and agreed to do as she said. He knew she was right.

They would still pray for Anna just like Anna had asked them to. And he would pray for what was really needed: a miracle.

Lilly followed behind Ahmad as they trekked through the palace.

They walked into the library, and as soon as Lilly entered, she knew she had been tricked. Her heart began beating wildly when she sensed that Anna was nowhere within the room.

Only the king stood before her, a smile on his lips.

Lilly turned around to run, but Ahmad grabbed onto her shoulders, holding her in place. "Ya lied to me!" she yelled at him, stomping her foot in fury.

She reluctantly turned toward the king as his voice rang out through the library. "The world is full of lies, my dear. The sooner you learn that, the better." He laughed coldly.

"What do ya want with me?" she asked him, her voice empty of all emotion.

"I *don't* want you," the king spat, "which is exactly why I have chosen to *use* you." He laughed again, causing chills to run up Lilly's spine.

At the king's command, Ahmad turned Lilly around and the king began to tie her hands together. She yanked herself free from Ahmad's grasp and turned around sharply, catching the king off guard. She turned to run, but Ahmad once again grabbed her.

"Let me go!" she demanded.

A sharp stinging to her face stopped her fight for the moment.

The king had slapped her.

Lilly didn't struggle as he grabbed her arms and tied them securely behind her back.

"Now," he hissed through his teeth, "you will be on your best behavior or you will regret it!" He then commanded her to walk, but she wouldn't budge. Her stubborn streak had come to its fullest. She refused to move an inch.

But the king refused to have that stop him, and with a quick command, he ordered Ahmad to carry her.

Ahmad picked her up and awkwardly slung her over his shoulder.

Lilly was still breathing heavily from fighting back. But she allowed herself to be carried, not wanting to even fathom where they could possibly be taking her.

Over and over again she murmured three words. *"Lord, help me."*

Caleb and his sisters sat around in a circle in his room after preparing for bed.

"We goin' to do our Scriptures now?" Margret asked, tilting her head to one side.

Caleb nodded and said that they were.

Their parents had taught them that reading the Bible and memorizing Scriptures was just as important as eating their daily food. They would die spiritually if they didn't have the meat of God's word every day.

Their parents had begun teaching them ever since they could speak, helping them to daily hide God's Word in their hearts.

They had also designed their own memory system, which the children were using now. They called it the, *Hear it, See it, and Write it* method. They also sang each memory verse to a different tune.

Each child set the necessary tools before them and happily began.

"Our verse for tonight is 1 John 4:18-19." Caleb said, then read it aloud.

*"There is no fear in love; but perfect love casteth out fear: because fear hath torment. He that feareth is not made perfect in love.
We love Him, because He first loved us."*

They set about writing their verse. Afterwards, they read it repeatedly and made up a tune that went with the verse. After they sang it through several times, they prayed together.

Julianna suggested that they play a game before bed.

"Let's play *Finish My Story!*" Margret begged.

They all agreed, and so the game began.

Caleb started the story and stopped at an exciting part. Then Julie started where he left off. Finally, it was little Margret's turn, which left them all in a fit of giggles. They kept on with the story until Mrs.

Banks called from downstairs and said that it was time for bed.

After telling each other goodnight, they each headed to their rooms.

Caleb climbed under the covers of his welcoming bed.

It wasn't very long until all of them, including Caleb, quietly slipped off to sleep.

Anna slowly stood up as she heard footsteps approaching her prison cell. It was the king. She knew his steps by now.

But there was also someone else with him.

Her heart caught in her throat as she noticed that the 'someone else' was Lilly.

"Lilly?" Anna spoke softly, her voice sounding unlike her own.

"Yes, aren't I nice?" King Raymond laughed, the sound sending chills up Anna's spine. "I brought your little friend to visit you!"

Anna's stomach churned and her hands trembled, palms growing sweaty. "What do you want with her?"

"It is not her I want, it's you."

Anna's brow crinkled in confusion. "Then what does she have to do with—" she stopped mid-sentence as it began to dawn upon her.

"Yes, I think you understand now," the king answered slyly, his voice edged with something Anna couldn't quite place.

Anna prayed she was wrong. The king stopped at nothing. He was cruel and merciless.

He stepped up the edge of her cell and wrapped his fingers around the cold lock, keeping hold of Lilly with his free hand.

The soft *click* of the key settling into the lock echoed through the cold dark prison, seeming to seal Anna's fate.

"You have three days to change your decision, or she dies!"

Raymond gave Lilly a slight shake and her eyes filled with intense fright.

This is too much! Anna thought as King Raymond opened the door of her cell and roughly shoved Lilly inside.

Anna caught Lilly before she landed on the hard stone floor.

This was all her fault. She had prepared herself for the death she knew was to come to her, but now Lilly's life was being threatened.

I don't know what to do, Lord! Anna begged silently, tears streaming down her face. *Please show me the way!*

Stephen was able to get away shortly after the king left the dark dungeon.

He had to find William. He had to tell him what was going on.

After a brief search, he found him in his room.

William showed his surprise as he ushered Stephen quickly into his room. "What happened?" He gasped, seeing Stephen's look of horror.

"He's threatening to take Lilly's life unless Anna renounces her faith." Stephen replied, breathing heavily from running up the flight of stairs.

William slowly sat down on his bed, his face in his hands.

"You scared me, Stephen!" he mumbled.

"But this is awful!" Stephen burst out, thinking William had grown heartless.

"Yes, it is." William replied. "Now we have two people to rescue instead of one."

Stephen didn't know what to make of William's comments.

"I've been thinking, Stephen." William said, looking up at him. "If we were able to find a ransom, would it be enough to get them out of there?"

Stephen nodded slowly. "It's happened before. One man stepping in to take the guilty man's place. But it would have to be a really important man, high in society, to be able to ransom both of them. And that man must be willing to give his life for them as well. I don't mean to be discouraging, but I don't think we can find that kind of man."

William sighed. He knew where to find him.

But was that man willing?

That was a question he couldn't yet answer.

Agnes was sitting on her favorite bench in the flower garden. She needed a change of scenery and had come out here to pray.

She prayed harder than she had ever prayed before. They needed a miracle, and they needed it fast. "Please, dear Lord!" she cried. "Help to conquer the battle of hatred going on inside my son. Humble him and take out his heart of pride. Change his ways, O Lord, if it be Your will...."

"I'm sorry, Lilly," Anna told her for the hundredth time since the king left almost three hours ago.

"It's not yer fault," was Lilly's continual answer. "I don't want ya to be renouncin' your faith, just 'cause of me."

Anna sighed. She knew she had no choice. She couldn't possibly renounce her faith, not for the sake of *her* life or Lilly's.

"I'm afraid I might hate the king, Anna," Lilly whispered, her tone full of worry. She knew hating someone was as terrible as murder, but she seemed to be losing the battle within her.

Anna admitted she too had struggled with the same thing. "But we just can't hate him, Lilly, we can't," she told her softly. "We must keep praying that the Lord will give us a heart full of pity for him and not hatred." Lilly nodded her agreement. All was quiet while both girls were lost in thought. But Anna's voice broke through the quietness. "I'm sorry, Lilly," she apologized again.

But Lilly knew this time, it was a different kind of *sorry.*

An apology, not for something she had done, but for something she had no choice but to do.

"I forgive ya, Anna," Lilly murmured, embracing her dear friend.

And she meant it. She meant it with all her heart.

Three days passed quickly for everyone within the palace.

On the last day, the king visited and told them they had one last chance to abandon their faith or she and Lilly would both die.

Anna boldly proclaimed for the third time that she had nothing to renounce.

The king walked away, calling her a fool.

As she and Lilly prayed together, a peace stole its way into their hearts. And Anna knew that whatever happened, whether they lived or died, they would be safe in the palm of their Savior's loving hand.

Twenty-one

 William walked through the passageway to the dungeon with determined steps. It was the only way, he told himself, and may God grant him the courage to do it.

"Stephen?" he called out, when he had arrived at the entrance of the prison.

"I'm here," Stephen answered, stepping forward into the light.

"I've found the man to ransom our captives," he said, his voice sounding squeaky and unlike his own.

"Who?" Stephen asked in surprise.

"He's right here," William answered.

Stephen looked confused. "Where?" he asked, looking behind William as he spoke.

"Right here," William said again, holding up his hands.

A light dawned upon Stephen's face.

"No, no, you don't mean—? You can't mean—?" Stephen stepped backwards, shaking his head, horror spreading over his face.

William nodded. "You said the man needed to be high in society and willing to die. Well, here I am," he said simply, though his heart was beating faster than he thought possible.

Stephen was still shaking his head.

"Bu-but William," he stuttered, "you would give yourself to die in their place?" He couldn't believe the sacrifice William was agreeing to.

William said he would. "It wasn't an easy decision to make, believe me, but it's something I know I must do."

Tears slid down Stephen's face as he embraced William.

"I would give my life," he cried, "but I'm not enough!"

William shook his head. "This is my decision, Stephen. Not yours."

Stephen stepped back. "Are you sure you want to do this?"

William took a deep breath and nodded. "I'm sure," he said, his voice full of determination.

Stephen opened the prison gate. "Wait here," he told him.

Stephen walked toward Anna's cell and soon he stood before them with the keys in his hand. "You're free to go," he said simply, though his heart was weeping.

Anna and Lilly's shocked expressions pressed him to explain. "Someone else has agreed to ransom you and go in your place," his voice trembled with emotion.

"Who?" Anna asked, her voice barely above a whisper.

Stephen slowly shook his head. He thought it best she didn't know.

Anna was in shock. She hadn't expected this to happen. Not that she hadn't expected God to answer her prayers, but she hadn't expected them to be answered like this.

She didn't know what to say as Stephen ushered them to the back door of the palace prison and paid the guard to take them to his mother's old house. "If anyone stops you, tell them you are on business for the king," he told all them, though it was only a half-truth.

The guard, who had been a dear friend of Jane's, nodded and obeyed without question.

"Stephen?" Anna stopped him before he had the chance to leave. "Please tell that person I shall never forget the sacrifice they made on our behalf—the little thanks I could offer would never be enough."

Stephen nodded and watched as they left with the guard. Slowly, he walked back to William, but his heart was filled with agony. He was rejoicing that Anna and Lilly were now free, but he was also mourning the fact he was about to lose a dear and beloved friend.

"Prepare the gallows," the king told the guard as he walked back to his room.

He'd had enough of Anna's pitiful games and was ready to get on with his life.

He was about to partake of his noonday meal which had just been brought in by a servant, when the guard returned.

"Everything is ready, Your Majesty," the guard informed him with a stiff bow. "Would Your Honor wish us to wait until you finish eating?"

The king shook his head. "Begin without me," he said. "I'll be there soon enough."

After he had eaten, he felt considerably tired and his head throbbed in pain. "What's come over me?" he slurred.

All the life and strength flew from his body as he staggered over to his bedside, falling over in a dead faint.

Stephen took William to the cell Anna and Lilly had just left and secured the lock.

He relayed Anna's message, and then left his post at the entrance of the prison. After a while, he returned to his post, his conscience burning heavily within.

Betty slowly limped up the stairs to her cabin, her hand resting lightly on her aching back.

She didn't feel sorry for Anna one bit, or at least that's what she said to convince herself. She got what she had coming to her. All she taught was from a book of lies, and Betty had witnessed that first hand.

She had given the coin to Anna because the verse said that if she gave, it would be given back to her. Not only the same amount, but much more. But what had she gotten? Nothing.

Betty sighed deeply as she lay on the cot in her cabin.

It was a lie, they were all lies. God wanted nothing to do with her.

Where was He when all her children were torn from her arms and sold out of her sight? Where was He when her husband, whom she loved even more than herself, died from being worked to death? Part of her died that day. From then on, she had wanted nothing to do with God. He didn't want anything to do with her either.

Betty didn't know how wrong those statements were, or how deeply He really cared for her.

She didn't know He was only a call away.

So she lay upon her cot, sulking in her grief, trying to convince herself that Anna's misfortune had nothing to do with her.

"Wake up, Your Majesty." Ahmad gently shook the king in the hopes of waking him from his stupor.

The king mumbled an incoherent reply as he slowly woke up.

His mind was hazy and he couldn't think properly. What had happened? He tried hard to remember.

He was fine until after he ate, but then he couldn't remember anything. Had he passed out?

Sitting up, he grabbed onto his head and moaned. What was Ahmad saying? He tried hard to listen.

"We believe you have been poisoned, Your Majesty," Ahmad said, his voice frozen and compassionless.

"Poisoned?" The king sat up, alert. "To what extent?"

"The doctor will be here soon, and he will be able to answer that question."

The doctor arrived shortly, a small, thin man with gray hair and glasses. He looked to be around seventy, but was still as spry as he was in his youth.

After the doctor examined him, he stepped back and nodded. "You are a very blessed man, Your Majesty, a very blessed man, indeed!"

The last thing the king felt was blessed, but he said nothing.

The doctor packed up his supplies while he continued to talk. "You have definitely been poisoned. To what extent, I cannot yet tell. It's a miracle you are still living. If you live through this, you should be back up and around in about a week or so. And I shall be back to check on you tomorrow, Your Highness." He turned toward Ahmad. "There is nothing we can do now but wait. Keep him fed and hydrated and we shall see what comes of it." With a nod and slight bow to the king, he left.

Ahmad soon left the king, and for that, Raymond was grateful. He needed time to think.

What was happening before he was poisoned?

The scullery maid! he thought, standing up and gripping the sides of his bed as he started to grow faint. Once he felt better, he walked over to the window. He had missed the hanging. How upsetting. After all he had done, he didn't even get the enjoyment of watching them die.

He sighed and looked bitterly out the window. A knock on his door interrupted his thoughts. Walking over to it, he opened it slowly. Before him stood a guard he had seen only a few times before.

The guard's face was deathly pale and he trembled in fear.

"Well, what do you want?" the king asked impatiently.

The guard, still trembling, relayed the message he had been sent to tell. "You-your son, Your Majesty," he stuttered.

The king gripped the doorframe, his knuckles turning white. "Well, what about him?"

The guard took a deep breath before continuing. "He ransomed the ladies who were imprisoned. Your son, he's-he's dead."

Anna took a deep breath, trying to calm her racing heart. But it was all in vain.

Stephen's friend had left them at her aunt's house a few hours ago, but neither Anna nor Lilly had stirred from their spot by the fire. They were tired, and terribly confused. But they were free; someone had taken their place!

But the joy she should have felt was not there.

I should feel happy, Anna thought. *I'm not going to be killed.* But the thought that someone out there was being killed in her place was almost too much to bear.

She should have stayed there. She should have insisted. But she'd been in shock and hadn't been able to think clearly.

After a few moments, Lilly broke the silence. "Jesus was also our ransom, ain't that right?" she asked. Her large brown eyes turned toward Anna, a look of thoughtfulness on her features.

Anna smiled as tears filled her eyes. "Yes," she said, her voice choking with emotion. "A much higher ransom than we shall ever deserve."

Epilogue

William awoke with a realization that something wasn't right. *Where am I?* He lifted his head and tried to look around. Everything was dark, nothing could be seen.

He heard muffled voices, and one he recognized as Stephen's.

He strained hard to listen.

"You shouldn't have done it, Stephen," said a masculine voice.

"I couldn't just stand there and watch William die! He didn't deserve any of this—it would have been absurd not to have done anything!"

"But you poisoned the *king*," the other voice answered. "You yourself could be killed because of it!"

"And I'm willing to take that risk, Job!" Stephen yelled, his voice filled with rage.

Silence reigned, but only for a moment.

"We aren't getting anywhere," Job said quietly.

Stephen didn't answer.

"What are you going to do with him?" Job asked, nodding his head toward the room William occupied. "He's been asleep for almost three days, but what are you going to do once he wakes up?"

"I don't know," Stephen replied. "Keep him quiet till this all dies down."

Job grunted derisively. "You poisoned the king and are keeping the prince hostage. What are you going to do next?"

Stephen stood up quickly. "I don't need your scorn, Job!"

William heard the scraping of a chair, and footsteps. Then a door slammed. William didn't know if it was Stephen or Job. But he didn't care, he had too much to think about.

His father was poisoned? He was taken here for what reason? And had he really been asleep for three days?

Stephen was just trying to help, he was sure. But he had gone too far this time.

William tried to remember how he had gotten here, but everything seemed hazy.

Where was he? What had happened to Anna and Lilly?

Was his father dead or alive?

Questions burned within William's mind, questions he had yet to match with answers.

All he could do was have faith, and be strong, and trust God with the uncertainty of his future.

"Play with me, Anna!"

Anna shook her head at Margret's plea and smiled apologetically. She brushed aside her little sister's hair as the wind blew it in her eyes. "A little later perhaps, mon chéri. Go inside and entertain Isaiah for a bit, I promise I'll play with you later."

Anna cringed at her little sister's downcast face. She realized with slight surprise that this was the first time she'd turned down one of her sibling's requests since she'd arrived back here in France almost a month ago.

But there was something she needed to do. Something she hadn't done religiously since she'd gotten back.

The clouds covering the sun moved slightly out of the way as Anna walked through the garden and up the small hill that held her parent's graves.

Walking through the grass, she smiled sadly as her view of the stone markers came into view.

Dropping down to her knees between the two stones, she traced her father's name and then her mother's. The rough stone was cool beneath her fingers.

She breathed deeply of the crisp air and pulled up a few stray weeds.

Her parents burial site was in the prettiest place.

Trees surrounded the entire area and a ring of flowers were planted around the stones in a large circle.

The flowers filled the air with the sweetest fragrance, but they were looking a little droopy, seeming to echo the feelings in Anna's soul.

"Oh, Papa, Mama. So much has happened since we last talked, I don't even know where to start."

A sad smile tipped the corners of Anna's mouth. "I've only come here twice in the last month and I'm sorry. I figured it was time to catch you up on a few things."

Tears pricked Anna's eyes, something she could never hold at bay whenever she visited this place.

"Lilly's still living with us and she's doing well. She's missing her mother though.

"I'm still trying to keep my anxieties away, but they seem to have a mind of their own. I'm positive that William was the one who took my place, and my heart seems to stop every time I think of it.

"What if he died and it was all my fault? How do I live with that?"

Anna's question was met with the rustling of leaves and the chirping of birds, the only answer she ever received in response to her questions during these conversations.

"Oh papa, I know if you were here you would say something like," Anna deepened her voice to match the low bass of her father's. "Now, Anna dear, let us hope and pray for the best. But as far as lessons are concerned, these feelings that you have should be the way we all feel about Jesus Christ. He died in *our* place. He was our willing Ransom."

Anna laughed quietly through her tears. "And I'll try to remember that, Papa."

She smoothed a wrinkle from her dress. "Lilly's a big help around the house, Mama. I'm trying to remember what you taught us about being hospitable, but Lilly's part of the family now. She insists on helping and I must let her, or else she would feel left out.

"We sold the farm, Papa. I know it was your pride and joy, but we couldn't maintain it any longer. There were too many things to tend to. I hope that was alright with you. I prayed about it a lot before we made the decision.

"We still kept our house though, because the buyer wanted to build his own at the edge of the property.

"Caleb took a job in town. He's a very hard worker and we rely heavily on his money to keep us going.

Anna glanced at the sky as it darkened considerably. Thunder began to rumble in the distance and she glanced down as a raindrop hit the back of her hand. "I have to leave now, but remember that we love you both and miss you dearly."

She stood and brushed the dirt from her apron, giving the graves one last look before turning around and making her way down the mountain.

Despite the unsettling feelings Anna had about her past, she knew without a doubt who held the future.

And she knew that the One who held the future was also the keeper of her heart.

Their God, their Messiah... their *Ransom.*

Dear reader:

This story wouldn't be complete if I failed to tell you that all stories don't end as sweet as Anna's did.
Many martyrs have given their lives for Christ's sake, not thinking of their own life, but proclaiming without fear the gospel of Jesus Christ.

Christian martyrs have been recorded from Biblical times; Andrew, James, Matthew, Jude and Peter, just to name a few. They all died for Christ's sake. In fact, eleven of the twelve apostles were martyred for their faith.

Edith Cavell, Polycarp and William Tyndale are some other Christian men and women who gave up everything for Christ, even to the point of death.

Jim Elliot is another touching story of pure faith and love for the lost.

But without doubt the most touching and inspiring martyr, the story which continues to amaze me no matter how many times I read it, is the story of Jesus Christ, who gave His very life for *us*. By no means will we ever be able to pay Him back, to thank Him enough for what He did by dying that cruel death, thinking not of Himself but only of others.

And now I come to the question every true Christian has or will encounter. *Would I give up my life for Christ?* It's a question I cannot answer for you, but a question that each Christian must determine within.

Are we willing to serve Christ without fear of man? Are we ready to advance the Kingdom of God for His glory? Are we ready to put on the Armor of God and go and fight for His sake? Are we ready to stand strong in our faith and preach the gospel to all generations?

Are we ready to die for Christ?

A Dim
Reflection

a novel by

ALEIGHA C. ISRAEL

A Dim Reflection

(Book Two)

William Caverly can't seem to understand the unsettling feeling that has been nagging him for far too long.

Memories of a baby sister are forever haunting his waking hours, and as he sleeps at night, he is repeatedly awakened by nightmares, confusing ones that he'd rather forget. He had been told that his baby sister died. He had seen her little body laid to rest beside their mother. But that didn't explain the dim remembrance that he had of an event that happened not too long after that.

Charlotte Porter's days are full and busy as she diligently teaches her young art students at her mother's boarding school, and tries desperately to stay away from an annoying suitor. Painting has been her passion and dream ever since she could hold a brush, but lately she has begun to question her mission and calling in life. What is her real purpose? And why does she know so little about her father, who supposedly died before she was born? William thinks he's discovered the hidden link that has kept him from his sister for over fifteen years. But then she's kid-napped, leaving William no choice except to find her and get her back. Once and for all.

A LIGHT FOR CHRIST TRILOGY

Book Three

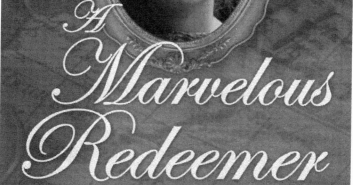

A
Marvelous
Redeemer

a novel by

ALEIGHA C. ISRAEL

A Marvelous Redeemer

(Book Three)

*She knew the decision would change her life.
But she didn't know she'd have to fight to
survive.*

When Amira put her faith in Christ, she knew
life wouldn't be easy. But hiding her conversion
from her Muslim family soon becomes the least
of her worries.

Forced to leave the only home she's ever
known, she travels to the island of
Gabeburough, trying her best to make a fresh
start.

Two escaped convicts and a treasure map. A
leafy paradise that becomes her home. Amira
begins to wonder, where is her Redeemer when
she needs Him the most?

Caleb Haddington is prince of Carpathia. Life
should be perfect, but he can't get a certain
dark-haired girl out of his mind. Amira was his
best friend when he lived in France, but her
letters to him have suddenly stopped.

Her last letter is filled with terror that her faith will soon be discovered.

Only a single hope keeps him alive; when the time is right, he's going after her. He'll bring her back and prove to the kingdom that he's a man. But the journey proves to be more perilous than he'd ever imagined. Ridicule, comfortless days and the threat of a hurricane are just the start of his problems.

Lying becomes easy for Caleb until his own life crumbles before him.

Brought to his knees under the pressure of his actions, he comes to realize the sweetness of his Savior.

Forgiveness, grace, and mercy are granted fully to those who ask.

Caleb and Amira soon discover that they don't just serve a gracious Savior, but a wonderful, magnificent, marvelous Redeemer.

ALEIGHACISRAEL.COM

VISIT TODAY!

Stay informed about
Aleigha C. Israel's
A LIGHT FOR CHRIST
TRILOGY

and more!

Bubble and Squeak

The origins of this dish are unknown, but it is firmly established in British culinary traditions. It's usually made to use up leftovers after a Sunday roast dinner, or a major holiday like Christmas.

Bubble and squeak is quintessentially British and makes for a hearty breakfast, lunch, or even a quick weeknight meal.

The unusual name stems from the bubbly and squeaky noises that the dish makes while being cooked.

This dish tastes wonderful just by itself, but it can also be served with fried eggs and sausages for a perfect meal.

Ingredients:

1 tablespoon butter
1 to 2 tablespoons canola oil
1/2 medium onion, finely diced
1/2 cup shredded, cooked brussel sprouts

1/2 cup shredded, cooked cabbage (optional)
1/2 cup grated carrots (can be cooked or raw)
2 cups leftover mashed potatoes
Salt and pepper to taste
Fried eggs, to serve (optional)

Method:

Gently heat the butter and oil in a wide, shallow skillet over medium heat. Add the onion. Cook for five minutes, until the onion is softened.

Turn up the heat to medium-high and add the shredded brussel sprouts, cabbage (if using), and carrots. Season with a little salt and pepper. Cook for five minutes, until the vegetables start to color.

Add the mashed potatoes to the skillet and stir briskly, until the vegetables and potatoes are well combined. Season again, to taste.

Press down on the skillet and fry for five to seven minutes, until the bottom is lightly browned and crisp. Drizzle a little oil around the edges if the mixture looks like it's drying out. The potato mixture should start making squeaking sounds at this point.

Using the lid of the skillet, invert the bubble and squeak into the lid, then slide back into the skillet to cook the other side. Cook for an additional five to seven minutes. Cut into wedges and top with fried eggs, if desired.

Recipe Notes:

- You can use almost any leftover vegetables to make bubble and squeak. Parsnips, peas, sweet potato mash and turnips all make excellent substitutes.
- You can also add bacon to this dish. Cook the bacon in the skillet first, then remove from the skillet, drain, and chop. Add a tablespoon of butter to the bacon fat and

continue as described, stirring in the chopped bacon with the potatoes.

The HSW Method
Hear It, See It, And Write It!

Did you know that when you memorize a song, it makes the words really hard to forget?

We have gone once a month for several years to an assisted living home, playing music and singing for the residents. You would be surprised at how many of those sweet residents still remember the words and tunes to so many of the songs that we sing.

Hearing the scriptures put to music is a key ingredient to easy memorizing.

So, upon that note, (no pun intended) let's get started!

Hear It:
Put music to the scriptures.

Take the verses that you would like to memorize and try putting music to them. It can be music from a song that you like or a completely made-up tune. It also helps if you split the verse into sections. I have put an example below:

I Corinthians 13:4
- Love suffers long and is kind
- Love does not envy
- Love does not parade itself
- Is not puffed up

Memorize each section of the verse and then add on another section. Before you know it you will have the entire verse memorized!

See It:
Take your verse and read it.
Over and over and over again. Read it using a strong inflection upon a different word each time. Put an exaggerated inflection on each bold word below:

- **Love** suffers long and is kind, love does not envy, love does not parade itself, is not puffed up.

- Love **suffers** long and is kind, love does not envy, love does not parade itself, is not puffed up.

- Love suffers **long** and is kind, love does not envy, love does not parade itself, is not puffed up.

- Love suffers long **and** is kind, love does not envy, love does not parade itself, is not puffed up.

Keep doing that until all the words have been used up. You will be amazed at how different it sounds, too! You might even learn something new by reading it that way.

Do that a few times until you are ready to move on.

Write It:

Get a piece of paper and copy your verse. Copy it at least five times. After that you should be able to write it almost without looking.

Well, that's all, folks!

Remember, don't get discouraged, and have fun! Memorizing God's Word is not only a fun thing to do, but it is also commanded:

"This Book of the Law shall not depart from your mouth, but you shall meditate in it day and night, that you may observe to do according to all that is written in it. For then you will make your way prosperous, and then you will have good success."
Joshua 1:8

"Let the word of Christ dwell in you richly in all wisdom, teaching and admonishing one another in psalms and hymns and spiritual songs, singing with grace in your hearts to the Lord."

Colossians 3:16

"I have not departed from the commandment of His lips; I have treasured the words of His mouth more than my necessary food."
Job 23:12

Memorize as many scriptures as you can. Believe me, they will soon come in handy!

Notes:

- It's important to memorize only one verse at a time. Once you have it down, then add another verse, saying both verse one and verse two one after the other.

- You may find it necessary to use only one part (Hear It, See It, or Write It) to memorize a scripture. For example, I can put a tune to the scripture and read it a few times, without having to write it down. Just play with it and see what works best for you.

- Remember, have fun and take joy in hiding God's Word in your heart!

Aleigha C. Israel

Scripture References

Romans 8:28
"And we know that all things work together for good to them that love God, to them who are the called according to his purpose."

John 14:27
"Peace I leave with you: my peace I give unto you: not as the world giveth, give I unto you. Let not your heart be troubled, neither let it be afraid."

1 Thessalonians 4:13-18
"But I would not have you to be ignorant, brethren, concerning them which are asleep, that ye sorrow not, even as others which have no hope.
For if we believe that Jesus died and rose again, even so them also which sleep in Jesus will God bring with Him.
For this we say unto you by the word of the Lord, that we which are alive and remain unto

the coming of the Lord shall not prevent them which are asleep.

For the Lord Himself shall descend from heaven with a shout, with the voice of the archangel, and with the trump of God: and the dead in Christ shall rise first:

Then we which are alive and remain shall be caught up together with them in the clouds, to meet the Lord in the air: and so shall we ever be with the Lord.

Wherefore comfort one another with these words."

Psalm 30:5

"For His anger endureth but a moment; in His favor is life: weeping may endure for a night, but joy cometh in the morning."

Psalm 28:8

"The Lord is their strength, and He is the saving strength of His anointed."

Psalm 145:20

"The Lord preserveth all them that love Him..."

Luke 10:25-37

"And, behold, a certain lawyer stood up, and tempted him, saying, Master, what shall I do to inherit eternal life?

He said unto him, What is written in the law? How readest thou?

And he answering said, Thou shalt love the Lord thy God with all thy heart, and with all thy soul, and with all thy strength, and with all thy mind; and thy neighbor as thyself.

And He said unto him, Thou hast answered right: this do, and thou shalt live.

But he, willing to justify himself, said unto Jesus, And who is my neighbor?

And Jesus answering said, A certain man went down from Jerusalem to Jericho, and fell among thieves, which stripped him of his raiment, and wounded him, and departed, leaving him half dead.

And by chance there came down a certain priest that way: and when he saw him, he passed by on the other side.

And likewise a Levite, when he was at the place, came and looked on him, and passed by on the other side.

But a certain Samaritan, as he journeyed, came where he was: and when he saw him, he had compassion on him,

And went to him, and bound up his wounds, pouring in oil and wine, and set him on his own beast, and brought him to an inn, and took care of him.

And on the morrow when he departed, he took out two pence, and gave them to the host, and said unto him, Take care of him; and whatsoever thou spendest more, when I come again, I will repay thee.

Which now of these three, thinkest thou, was neighbor unto him that fell among the thieves?

And he said, He that shewed mercy on him.

Then said Jesus unto him, Go, and do thou likewise."

Jeremiah 29:11

"For I know the thoughts that I think toward you, saith the Lord, thoughts of peace and not of evil, to give you an expected end."

2 Timothy 4:6-8

"For I am now ready to be offered, and the time of my departure is at hand.

I have fought a good fight, I have finished my course, I have kept the faith: Henceforth there is laid up for me a crown of righteousness, which the Lord, the righteous judge, shall give me at that day: and not to me only, but unto all them also that love His appearing."

Matthew 10:28
"And fear not them which kill the body, but are not able to kill the soul: but rather fear Him which is able to destroy both soul and body in hell."

John 11:25
"Jesus said unto her, I am the resurrection, and the life: he that believeth in me, though he were dead, yet shall he live."

1 John 3:17
"But whoso hath this world's good, and seeth his brother have need, and shutteth up his bowels of compassion from him, how dwelleth the love of God in him?"

Luke 6:38
"Give, and it shall be given unto you; good measure, pressed down, and shaken together, and running over, shall men give into your

bosom. For with the same measure that ye mete withal it shall be measured to you again."

Matthew 19:26
"...With God, all things are possible..."

John 16:33
"These things I have spoken unto you, that in me ye might have peace. In the world ye shall have tribulation: but be of good cheer; I have overcome the world."

Philippians 4:6-7
"Be careful for nothing; but in everything by prayer and supplication with thanksgiving let your requests be made known unto God. And the peace of God, which passeth all understanding, shall keep your hearts and minds through Christ Jesus."

Matthew 11:28-30
"Come unto me, all ye that labor and are heavy laden, and I will give you rest. Take my yoke upon you, and learn of me; for I am meek and lowly in heart: and ye shall find rest unto your souls.
For my yoke is easy, and my burden is light."

Psalm 16:11

"Thou wilt shew me the path of life: in thy presence is fullness of joy; at thy right hand there are pleasures for evermore."

2 Corinthians 5:6-8

"Therefore we are always confident, knowing that, whilst we are at home in the body, we are absent from the Lord. For we walk by faith, not by sight. We are confident, I say, and willing rather to be absent from the body, and to be present with the Lord."

2 Chronicles 7:14

"If my people, which are called by my name, shall humble themselves, and pray, and seek my face, and turn from their wicked ways; then will I hear from heaven, and will forgive their sin, and will heal their land."

1 John 4:18-19

"There is no fear in love; but perfect love casteth out fear: because fear hath torment. He that feareth is not made perfect in love.
We love Him, because He first loved us."

John 14:6

"Jesus saith unto him, I am the way, the truth, and the life: no man cometh unto the Father, but by me."

Philippians 2:10 (NKJV)
"That at the name of Jesus every knee should bow, of those in heaven, and of those on earth, and of those under the earth."

The Highest Honor

© *Aleigha C. Israel*

"To give up your life for Christ,
Is something few would choose to do,
To share the blessed story
Even when it becomes dangerous to pursue,
They care not of themselves,
But others and their souls lost to their god,
Not even when thinking twice that it could
end
With their body beneath the sod,
For to die for Christ would be such an
honor,
And they're excited to share His story,
Even if it means death on their behalf,
To them they deem it glory,
There are but few who would give their life
For sharing a story about Gods love,
But as they're martyred for their faith,
They'll soon be smiling up above."

95882254R00200

Made in the USA
Columbia, SC
18 May 2018